Introduction

Meechie lay back on the sofa in the living room of the small apartment that she shared with her best friend and roommate Carmen, her cell pressed against her ear. "Boy, quit lying." She giggled into the phone, biting on her bottom lip.

"Girl, I ain't bullshitting you!" Rodney laughed. "I do big shit and make big moves! I ain't like that nigga that you used to fuck with! Considered yo'self upgraded!"

Meechie rolled her eyes up in her head. She had been *dating* Rodney for a little over a month now and the one thing that irked her nerves about him was his arrogant attitude. He was always bragging about the things that he had and the moves that he was making. Yeah, he did his thing and handled his business but that wasn't something that she wanted to talk about 24/7. She never said anything to him about it though because he kept her pockets laced, bills paid, hair and nails done and she stayed dressed in something fly! He was on the phone now promising that he was going to get her a new whip. She knew that he could afford it. Him and his cousin Demetrius kept Jordan City flooded with dope. Their paper was indeed long and there wasn't a bitch in Jordan City who didn't want to get with them in hopes of "coming up". That was her reason for dealing with him. He was cool and all but if he wasn't getting money then she would've never looked his way. She was hoping that now she could finally quit her job at Walmart and stay at home all day and do whatever she wanted instead of having to be worried about punching somebody's clock. That shit just wasn't for her! She had grown up watching her mama struggle, working a minimum wage job, living paycheck to paycheck always worried about how she was going to pay the bills and keep food on the table. She didn't want that life! She wanted to be worry free and live like a queen or at least live comfortably.

"Okay, we gone see."

"Look, you're my girl now and if you are fucking with me then you are always going to have the best! I can't have you driving around in that old beat up ass Camry that you drive!" He continued to laugh. "Hell nah, I have an image to uphold girl. I been wanting to fuck with you for a minute Meechie on some real shit but you were all stuck on Shad's bum ass! It's all good though because now that you're mine, I'm going to show you how a real man is supposed to treat his woman. You deserve nothing but the best girl and you are going to have that. That's my good word! You are a beautiful woman and you shouldn't have to be worried about how you are going to eat or pay bills and from now on you won't have to worry about that. I got you."

Meechie rolled her eyes up in her head again for like the twelfth time since they'd been on the phone. She didn't give a damn about his image or any of that other stuff that he was yapping about as long as she got a new car! She was tired of the one that she had because it seemed like every time she got one thing fixed on it something else would happen. Her ex- Shad had bought her that car over a year ago from one of his homeboys so that she could have a way back and forth to work instead of having to catch rides and pay other people. At the time she'd been happy as hell to finally have her own transportation even if it wasn't the flyest ride, it was hers. It had a big dent in the back on the passenger side from where his homeboy had wrecked it and the passenger side mirror was taped on with grey duct tape, which stuck out like a sore thumb because the car was red. To top it all off the motor made a loud rattling noise. She was more than ready to be rid of that ugly ass car but on the flipside she didn't want to totally be rid of it because Shad had given it to her. She just wanted a new one and she would keep that one. It was paid for and it could always be her plan B if the new one messed up.

"So when am I going to get my car?" Meechie asked wiggling her toes, thinking to herself that she was in need of a pedicure.

"We can go look at some cars this weekend if you want." Rodney responded.

"That's..." BOOM...BOOM...BOOM! Somebody was banging at the front door like there was an emergency! Meechie jumped up, heart racing from being startled! "Hold on Rodney." She didn't wait for a response. She dropped the phone down on the sofa and ran to the door. She looked through the peephole and saw Shad standing on the other side of the door. He banged again. He was banging so hard that the pictures on the wall next to the door shook. She could tell by the expression on his face that he was upset about something.

"Damn, what in the hell is your problem?" Meechie asked as she swung open the door and was face to face with a visibly upset Shad.

His nose was flared and his chest heaved up and down. His eyes were red and looked deranged. The wife beater that he wore was soaked and so was his face because it had been raining all night. He didn't have a car so he had walked to her place. "Yo, you fucking Rodney?" He barked pointing his finger in Meechie's face!

4

"Huh?" Was the first thing to slip from her lips even though she'd heard perfectly clear what he'd asked. "What is wrong with you coming up in here tripping and pointing your finger in my face?" She smacked his hand trying to knock it out of her face but it didn't budge. She was also trying to buy some time to figure out whether or not she should be straight up with him about Rodney or lie.

He stepped closer in her face. "Answer my fuckin' question!" This time his finger poked her in her forehead causing her head dipped back!

"Why?" She asked still trying to avoid answering the question. She'd never seen him this upset before and she was afraid of what he might do if she said the wrong thing. He stood 6'2, weighing 198lbs. He had a natural muscular build and was cut like he worked out every day. His huge hands could snap her little neck with little or no effort. She was only 5'2 and 132lbs. There was no way that she could defend herself against him without a weapon.

Shad could tell by her reaction to his question that the things he'd been hearing about her and Rodney were true. It hurt him to his heart to find out that the girl that he'd loved for the past five and a half years would not only walk out on the love that he thought the two of them shared but then to fuck with his cousin made it much worse. "Bitch, I can't believe your trifling ass!"

Meechie was stunned to hear Shad call her out of her name, something that he'd never done before. They'd had some bad arguments during their relationship but never once had he put his hands on her or called her out of her name. "Bitch?" She repeated hoping that she'd just heard him wrong.

"You heard me! That's exactly what you are! How you gone fuck my cousin...my cousin Meechie! Gotdamn! It's a city full of niggas and you chose my folks!" He shook his head giving her a disgusted look. "What kind of fucked up shit are you on? First you come at me talking about you need some space because shit just wasn't working for you anymore..."

She'd heard enough and the guilt of knowing that she had violated by fucking his cousin was eating at her. She tried to defend herself. "It wasn't working for me anymore Shad! I got tired of always struggling and trying to make ends meet! Always worried about how I was going to pay a bill, never having any money left for myself, never able to go out and buy myself anything! Shit I want to have nice things too! I deserve it dammit! You act like you are scared to step your game up and hustle like these other niggas! They are taking a chance every day but they do it because don't nobody want to be fucked up struggling..."

"Will you listen to the dumb shit coming out of your mouth? Like you said they are taking a chance every day for bullshit like cars, rims, clothes and jewelry! Fuck that! Shad ain't going out like that! Have you forgotten that my brother is doing ten years right now behind that fast money! That's ten years that he can't ever get back! What you so thirsty to keep up with these project bitches that you want me to risk gettin' locked up?"

Meechie shifted her weight from one foot to the other and folded her arms across her chest. With her head cocked to one side she looked up at him and asked. "Why do you always have to bring up Shannon? He was stupid and doing all types of crazy shit, living reckless that's why he got caught but you are way smarter than that."

Shad couldn't believe that this was *his* Meechie talking. It was like he didn't even know this woman that was standing before him. He ran his hands over his wet face and looked at her shaking his head. He looked into her eyes searching them for the woman that he once knew, the one that loved him with all of her heart and soul, the one that didn't give a damn whether he had two dollars or two million dollars. He didn't see her. When he spoke this time it was in a much calmer tone. "I don't know what happened to you but you are not the woman that I fell in love with. I stood here and listened to all of the reasons why you were tired of being with me. You named several things that you *wanted* that I couldn't provide but never once did you name anything that you *needed* that I didn't provide. I may not have a lot of money but I shared with you everything that I have. Anything that you needed I made sure that you had it. I realize now that you can give your all to some people but it will never be enough. I won't stand here and tell you that it doesn't hurt the fuck out of me to know that you can put a price on our love or at least the love that I thought we shared because it does. It's all good though, one day you're going to realize that money, cars, clothes, jewelry, and hood fame ain't everything." After saying his piece he turned and walked away.

Meechie ran after him not caring about the fact that she didn't have on any shoes. She didn't want things to end this way. The look of hurt that she'd just seen in his eyes tugged at her heart. She didn't want him thinking of her as some gold-digging hoochie because it wasn't like that. That's not the way that she saw it at all. She just wanted a little bit more than what she had. What was so wrong with that? "Shad...Shad..." She called after him but it only fell on deaf ears. He didn't want to hear shit else that she had to say. "Shad, I know that you hear me calling you!" she screamed as she walked behind him across the wet parking lot. Her doobie wrap that she'd just gotten done earlier that day was now ruined but she didn't care. She needed to try and get him to see things from here point of view. Maybe she'd chosen to walk away from their relationship for selfish reasons but that didn't change the fact that she did love him. "Shad!"

He kept walking, ignoring her calls. She'd changed and he wanted nothing to do with the superficial bitch that she'd become. With each step that he took he grew angrier and angrier. Here he was walking because he'd taken part of the money that he'd been saving up and bought her a car so that she could get back and forth to work and this was the thanks that he got! She walked out on him because he wasn't ballin' out of control, pushing a fly whip or able to keep her laced in all of the hottest gear. He'd given her something way more valuable than all of the bullshit that Rodney was showering her with! He'd given her his heart and loved her unconditionally, always putting her needs before his own. His boys often teased him that he was too soft when it came to Meechie but he never gave a damn about any of that because he was his own man. He wasn't a follower! He was a leader! He felt like his woman deserved to be treated like a queen.

"Shad will you please stop for a second and just hear me out! Please!" Meechie called as they crossed the playground. Her feet were wet and muddy. She stepped in a puddle causing water to splash on her legs. "Fuck!" She yelled. "Shad, for real you are trippin! I don't have on any shoes and I've gotten my hair wet! Come on!"

He stopped walking and spun around. "What? What do you want?" He barked. Water ran down his face, arms and chest. The rain was still coming down really hard.

Meechie stood in front of him, the hair products in her hair mixed with the rain that ran down her face some getting into her eyes. "Damn!" She wiped her eyes with her hands.

"What do you want?" Shad repeated not caring that something was obviously wrong with her eyes.

"Hold on! This stuff from my hair got in my eyes!" She shouted agitated that he was acting like such an ass! He turned and started walking again. She took off after him grabbing a hold of his shirt! "Wait! Why are you being like this?" She blinked because the chemicals were still burning her eyes.

"Get your hands off of me!" He snatched away from her. "How am I supposed to be? You tell me!"

Meechie dropped her head. "Shad, I'm sorry. I never meant to hurt you…"

He let out a sarcastic chuckle. "Are you serious? C'mon man, you can't be! What you thought that I was going to be ecstatic to find out that you were fucking my cousin?"

"No…no…Shad that's not what I meant!" She moved her hair back out of her face and looked up at him. "I meant that…I just wanted more than what you could give me. I kept trying to tell you that I wasn't happy but for some reason you weren't hearing me. I ain't ever had shit since I was a kid and I am at the point in my life where I want to have something better!"

Hearing those words only angered him more! "That's the point of hard work! You're right, you want more but you don't want to work hard to get more! You think that shit is just supposed to be given to you! That ain't the way that shit works! You have to bust your ass to get what you want in this world! Ain't shit given to nobody and I do mean nobody! You are just like most of these dumb ass niggas out here in the hood always thinking of a quick come up but never taking the time to think about the consequences of it! That fast money don't bring nothing but fast time or worse! Don't get me wrong it's good while you are getting it and everything is gravy but what about when that shit catch up to your ass, then what?" He didn't wait for her to respond he continued. "You've been begging me for a minute to go out here and hustle but I am so glad that I didn't listen to your ass because you have proven what you would've done as soon as I got locked up or some nigga caught me slippin' and rob and killed my ass! You would've been on to the highest bidder!"

His words hurt. They cut her really deep. Without a second thought she slapped the shit out of him! "So what are you saying nigga? You think that I am a hoe or something?"

He took her slap like a man. "If the shoe fits!" He shot back and turned to walk away again.

Meechie ran behind him her tiny fists raining blows all over his back, calling him every name in the book! "Fuck you! You stupid motherfucka! I don't give a fuck what you think of me! You just mad because I've moved on and left your broke ass! You mad because Rodney is doing what you couldn't nigga! He makes me happy and..."

He'd taken a lot of things from Meechie and walked away like a man but there was no way he was going to allow her to continue to disrespect him like this! It was bad enough that she was fucking his cousin but if she thought that her trifling ass was going to boast about it then she had another thing coming. He turned around and pushed her hard sending her stumbling backwards and falling on her ass onto the muddy wet ground! "I started to knock fire from your ass but I am too much of a man to lay my hands on you! Keep testing me though and you are going to see a side of me that you don't want to!" He roared. "Stay the fuck away from me and I promise you that I will give you the same courtesy!" he turned and left her sitting on the ground.

"Fuck you, Shad!" She yelled at his back!

Meechie

A week has gone by since the argument with Shad and I. In a way I feel kind of bad because of the way that things went down but what can I do? What's done is done. I can't change it so I just have to forget about him and move on. I mean he's playing victim and all like I just woke up, decided to leave him and fuck with Rodney all over night! That's not at all how things happen! He needs to take some responsibility in all of this. I've been trying to tell him for a while that I wasn't feeling our situation. Especially after we got evicted from our place because we couldn't afford to pay the bills! He knows that me and my people don't get along. Carmen was nice enough to open her door up to me and allow me to stay with her. So far everything has been Gucci but I don't plan on being there much longer either. I want my own spot with my name on the lease! Shad will be okay! He's got the game fucked up! The way I see it is that the man is supposed to be the provider! I shouldn't have to worry myself about how bills are going to be paid or how we are going to eat! He should already have that shit figured out and then grease my palms with a few hundred so that I can have some money left to spend on myself but he's so afraid of catching a case that he'd rather work at that lil whack ass detailing shop making minimum wage! I love him and he will always have a special place in my heart but it's time for me to do me!

I am sitting up under the dryer waiting for my roller set to dry, flipping through the pages of a Sister to Sister magazine and I come across an article on Tyrese Gibson. I roll my eyes and turn the page. I've always thought that Shad resembles Black Ty, same complexion and everything. The only difference is Shad keeps his hair cut close. He doesn't do the bald thing. I come across another article on Lil' Wayne and start to read. I am so wrapped up in the article that I don't even see Jada walk in. She and I have had beef for a few years now. It's not to the point where we argue or fight every time that we see each other. We have what you might call a silent understanding. As long as that hoe stays in her lane everything will be good!

She used to have a thing for Shad. About four years ago, he and I were at a party thrown by one of his homeboys. I was of doing my thing with my girls and allowing him some space to kick it with the fellas. I've never been the clingy type all up my man's ass. Jada must not have seen me or maybe she did know I was there and just didn't care! I just so happen to look across the room and see her skeezer ass is all up in my man's grill. I walked over to where they were and tapped her on the shoulder. "Ummm...excuse me but would you mind backing the hell up off of my man?" I asked my speech a little bit slurred because I'd had a few shots of Henny.

She turned to look at me with her nose turned up; her light grey eyes looking me up and down like I was a piece of shit! "Little girl why don't you go back over there with your little friends or crawl back into whatever liquor bottle that you crawled out of!" She turned back to Shad. "Boo you need to let me upgrade you. She's out here smelling like a wino and looking like a two dollar hoe! You shouldn't be parading no chick like that around on your arm! You need a real woman, one with some respect for herself and you!"

"Yo baby girl, you need to watch your mouth when you are talking about my girl. Real talk that shit ain't cool and it's very unattractive. Throwing salt on her don't get you nowhere with me." Shad straightened her ass before I had a chance.

She placed her hands on her wide hips. "I ain't throwing salt! I'm stating facts!" She swiveled her neck.

"Bitch!" I lunged at her grabbing a hand full of her naturally curly light brown hair. I had her hair wrapped around my hands and was raining blows on her head and face! There was no way that this hoe was about to play me in front of my man and everybody that was at the party and get away with it! She'd asked for the ass whooping that I was putting on her ass! In the mist of us fighting the short yellow mini skirt that I was wearing ended up around my waist exposing my yellow lace thong. I could hear niggas whistling and hollering but I didn't give a damn about them seeing my ass! If you've seen one ass you've seen them all! I continued to mop the floor with Jada until Shad and his boy Toby broke it up. After that whenever Jada would see me or see me and Shad together she would look in the other direction. That ass whooping had served its purpose! It'd let her know to stay in her lane and not to bother stepping out unless she was prepared to deal with the consequences!

I look up just as Jada is taking a seat in Felicia's chair. Our eyes meet briefly and I roll mine hard enough to cross them. I look back down at the magazine that I am reading but can't really get back into the article because seeing her has messed up my entire vibe. I hear Felicia ask Jada what she is getting done to her hair.

"I want it washed, deep conditioned and straightened." She replies.

"Alright." Felicia says and then asks Jada to get up and walk over to the sink so that she can wash her hair.

I can't take anything from Jada, she's a bad bitch! She has a body like a video vixen. Her breasts look to be at least some C cups, with a small waist, wide hips and an ass that would put Nicki Minaj to shame! She has long naturally curly brown hair that hangs mid-way of her back. Her eyes are light grey and she has a slender little pointy nose with full lips and skin the color of caramel. She could be a model with no problem. The only thing that messes her up is the fact that she thinks that she is better than everybody else. She graduated high school with honors and attended Jordan Community College for a few years. She recently opened her own café downtown last year. I hear that she has a nice crib downtown as well in an all-white neighborhood and she drives a pearl white 2011 Chevy Impala. I'm not a hater because she's done good for herself but that doesn't make that bitch any better than me!

Chantel comes over to the dryer where I am sitting and lifts the top to check my hair. "Alright mama, you are good let me take these rollers out of your hair." I place the magazine back on the table beside the dryer where I got it from. Then I get up and follow her over to her station and get in the chair. "Girl, that's a cute outfit that you're wearing. Where did you get it?" She asks referring to the orange and purple Baby Phat halter jumper that I am wearing with a pair of orange Baby Phat gladiator sandals to match.

"I got this from the mall from that new store that just opened call Urban Fashions." I look in the mirror at her as we are talking and she is taking the rollers out of my hair.

"Well it's cute. Did they have any other colors? I would like something with some pink in it. Pink is my favorite color." That isn't something that she needed to tell me because whenever I come in here she is always wearing pink. I've never seen her without something pink on. Her car is even pink.

"Yeah I believe they had some pink and white ones."

"That's what's up." I can see Felicia applying conditioner to Jada's hair through the mirror. The two of them are carrying on their own little conversation.

"Girl, I am going to have to stop by your café sometimes and check it out. I haven't been in there since when you first opened it." Felicia tells Jada.

Jada laughs. "Yeah, you need to come through and check us out. I am really proud of how good business has been. We have a lot more going on now than we did before. We have a wide selection of books. You can come in and get your read on and relax. We serve different kinds of sandwiches, salads, pastries, baked goods, coffee, tea, smoothies. We also have different events like poetry nights, karaoke nights, and live jazz bands. It's really nice and laid back. You definitely have to come through and check us out."

I roll my eyes again and suck my teeth. It was just like her ass to start bragging as soon as Felicia mentioned her little funky ass café. That shit probably isn't all of that!

"Be nice!" Chantel whispers to me knowing about the situation between me and Jada.

"I can't stand that chick, I swear! She's just so damn bouji!" I mumble back and began to mock Jada. "*We have special sandwiches, tea and coffee. Jesus is there as well every Friday night! Everybody who is anybody comes by my café!*"

Chantel bursts into laughter. "Girl quit! You are so damn crazy." She says as she styles my hair, pinning up my curls on one side.

"I'm serious. She works my damn nerves." I am still looking at Jada through the mirror hoping that she hears me and says something so that I can whoop her ass again but she isn't even looking in my direction. She is still bragging to Felicia.

"Damn that does sound nice!" Felicia is acting as if her ass has never been to a café before. "I'm going to try and stop by there soon. Hopefully I will stop through on poetry night. I love me some poetry girl."

"Oh really?" Felicia has put a plastic cap on Jada's hair and is now sitting down beside her. "Well the next poetry night is two weeks from now on a Tuesday. It starts at 8 and ends at 12. I would love for you to come."

"Alright I certainly will try to make it!" The two of them continue to chat. After Chantel finishes with my hair I take a look in the mirror and is very pleased with my do, I thank her, pay and then leave.

I'm glad that I chose to park on the side of the hair salon because I don't want Jada seeing me get in this raggedy ass car! I get to my car and toss in my Baby Phat bag and then get inside. I check my hair in the mirror once more before slipping on my shades and then backing out of the parking lot. I am on my way up Arlington Blvd. when I take out my cell and dial Rodney. It rings a few times before he answers. It sounds like there is a party going on in the background. The music is loud and a lot of loud laughing and talking is going on. His baritone voice booms through the phone like he is trying to talk over the noise. "Hey baby. What's good?"

"Ain't much going on my way. A sista is a little hungry so I was hoping that we could meet somewhere and grab something to eat." I suggest. We don't get the opportunity to spend much time together being that he is always *making moves.* I'm not complaining because him doing what he has to do is how he is able to give me the things that I want but I don't want him thinking that it's all about the money either.

"Yeah we can do that." He agrees. "Where are you at now?"

"I'm over on Arlington Blvd. about to turn on Fredrick St." I respond putting on my signal and making a right onto Fredrick St. "Where you at?"

I hear him tell somebody in the background to hold on. "I'm about to leave Demetrius' crib. Where do you want to eat at? What do you have a taste for?"

The background noise is getting on my nerves because he is pretty much screaming in my ear. "Let's meet at Lonnie's Seafood. I have a taste for some crab stuffed ravioli."

"Aight Lil' Mama, I'll be there in fifteen." He agrees.

"Aight, see you then." We hang up and I head over to Lonnie's Seafood. I arrive at Lonnie's and inform the hostess that I will be needing a table for two. He grabs two menus and silverware and asks me to follow him. He tries to seat me at a table near the front. "Ummm...I'd prefer a table further back." I say him.

"That's no problem at all ma'am, follow me." He leads the way and I follow him to a booth at the back of the restaurant that is near the window. "Is this alright?"

"Yes this is fine." I smile and take a seat.

He places the menus and silverware on the table. "Your waitress will be Melody. She will be with you shortly." He smiles revealing a mouth full of braces before turning and walking away.

A few minutes pass before a young girl that looks to be in her early twenties approach my booth. "Hi, I am Melody and I will be your waitress for the evening. Would you like to order something to drink?"

"Ummm...yes, can I have two sweet teas with lemon please?"

"Yes ma'am, would you like to go ahead and order as well?"

"No, I'll wait until my boyfriend arrives." I smile politely.

"Alright, I'll be back shortly with your drinks." She leaves and I sit staring out the window at the street. Shad crosses my mind but I quickly push all thoughts of him out of my head. I look across the restaurant just in time to see Rodney walking my way. I smile because he is looking extra sexy in a pair of black Polo jeans, a black and white Polo shirt and a pair of black Polo shoes. He is a little on the thick side but he's not sloppy with it. He's solid. He has paper bag brown skin, with a bald head and sports a beard like Rick Ross on his face.

He reaches the table, leans over and kisses me before sitting down. "Damn girl you are looking good enough to eat!" He compliments me smiling. I absolutely hate the fact that the entire front of his mouth, top and bottom, is decorated with gold teeth. I normally am not attracted to men with grills but with how good he treats me I am willing to overlook it.

The waitress returns and sits our drinks in front of us before I have a chance to respond to Rodney's compliment. "Here are your drinks. Do you need a few more minutes to look over the menu or do you already know what you would like to order?"

"I already know." I answer and then look over at Rodney. "Baby, do you need a few more minutes?"

He runs his hand over his beard. "Nah, I want the fried trout with a baked potato and green beans."

The waitress writes down his order before looking at me. "And what would you like ma'am?"

"I want the crab stuffed ravioli with a piece of garlic bread." I reply folding my menu and handing it to her. She writes down my order and then takes both menus. "Okay let me go and put these in for you. Your food should be ready in about fifteen to twenty minutes."

"That's what's up." Rodney responds.

She leaves and I look across the table at Rodney who is also looking back at me as if he is undressing me with his eyes. "Thank you, baby for the compliment. Do you like my hair?"

"Yeah it looks nice."

"Thanks, I just got it done."

"You are looking sexy as usual." He says.

"Well I try." I say touching my hair lightly. "You know I have to try and stay fly. I can't have them other chicks up in Walmart looking better than me."

"Have you thought anymore about what we talked about the other night?"

"What about me going back to school?"

"Yeah."

"Yeah I've thought about it." I lied. "I don't know though."

"What do you mean, you don't know? You are always complaining about having to work at Walmart. You could go right there to JCC and take some courses and learn some type of trade so that you won't have to work in Walmart. I told you that I would pay for it."

"Alright baby, I'll check into it." I say just to shut him up. I have no intentions what so ever on going back to school. I didn't even want to go when I had to and I know damn well I'm not going to go back!

"I saw your boy today. I went over to the shop where he works to have my truck cleaned up. That nigga was walking around like he has a chip on his shoulder or something." Rodney chuckles. "You had better tell him to get his mind right before I have to bust his shit! Ain't no need for him to be walking around with his panties in a bunch over no broad! When he had you he didn't step up to plate and handle his business so he needs to build a bridge and get the fuck over it! I ain't the nigga that he wants to come at the wrong way!" He looks at me as if to say he is warning me. "He's carrying it like him and me were tight or something and I took him woman. We have never been tight. When we see each other we speak but that's about it. It's not like him and I ever hung out. We run in two totally different circles."

I am slightly offended by him referring to me as a *broad* and I let him know it! "Okay first and foremost, I ain't no broad! Secondly, I asked you to meet me here so that we could have dinner and spend some time together, not talk about Shad! If there was something that you needed to get off of your chest then you should've done it when you was down at the shop face to face with him! Not wait until you get here and throw the shit up in my face, okay?" My mood has been ruined just that quickly.

His entire demeanor changes and the expression on his face looks like he may come across the table and slap the piss out of me! He sits up. "Yo baby girl, I don't know what type of lames that you are used to but you'd better check how the fuck you be talking to me! I ain't no lil pussy nigga that you can just talk to any way that you fucking feel like! In other words, I ain't Shad! Furthermore, don't get it twisted! I will tell that nigga anything that I have to tell him! Who the fuck is he? The only reason I am telling you to check your boy is because I ain't much of a talker! You know what I mean?"

This motherfucker has the audacity to try and check me! That ain't even about to go down! "Hold up! Who in the fuck do you think you are talking to?"

"You, that's who!" He stands up getting loud. "I told you, I ain't Shad the shit that you did with him ain't gone fly with me! Don't no bitch spend my money and then thinks that she is going to disrespect me! You got the game fucked up! As a matter of fact, I'm out!" He reaches in his pocket, pulls out a wad of money and peels off a hundred dollar bill and tosses it on the table. "Enjoy the rest of your meal! I don't have time for this bullshit! Call me whenever you get your mind right or should I say when you get out of your feelings. Seems to me like you mad because I said something about your boy! If you are that concerned about that nigga then maybe that's who you need to go be with!" With that he leaves.

I am left sitting here looking stupid and wondering what the fuck just happened.

Rodney

I leave the restaurant mad as fuck because as usual Meechie doesn't know

what the fuck to say out of her mouth! I don't feel like I disrespected her in any

kind of way. She trippin' because I called her a broad! Shit that's just the way I

talk! She knows that I didn't mean anything by it. It's not like I called her a bitch!

Honestly I don't think that she is upset by me calling her a broad, I think that she

just put it off on that. I think that she got heated because I was talking about

Shad's punk ass! Personally I don't have anything against him but at the same

time he's not going to be looking at me like he wants to do something when he

sees me! If he feels some type of way about me fucking with Meechie, that's his

problem! I didn't steal her! She's a grown ass woman who makes her own

decisions. When we started talking she told me that the two of them weren't

together anymore so I don't understand what the problem is. The only reason

that I mention anything to her about what happened was because like I said back at the restaurant, I'm not much of a talker. I don't give a damn about him being my folks! I will put something hot in his ass if he comes at me the wrong way!

I turn left onto Pine St. and as soon as I do I nearly hit this young redbone crossing the street, who clearly isn't paying attention. I slam on brakes and blow my horn! My heart is beating rapidly against my chest because I almost hit her ass and because I am riding dirty! This could've been a real fucked up situation just now! I roll down the window. "Yo what the fuck are you doing?" I yell. "You need to pay attention before someone hits your ass!"

Her eyes are big as hell and she looks scared to death. She has her hand over her heart, probably because it's beating just as fast as mine! "I-I...didn't s-see you. I am s-so s-s-sorry." She stutters visibly shaken up. She looks to be somewhere around sixteen or seventeen years old. She has a tight little body on her, very petite but curvy. I can't help but notice how phat she is in the skintight jeans that she is wearing. She has a really cute face too, round with a wide nose, full lips and light brown eyes.

My anger lessens some after seeing how shaken up she is. "Yeah well you need to pay better attention. You're too fine to be getting scraped up off the pavement."

She lets out a nervous laugh, still holding her chest. "Yeah I guess you're right." She crosses the street and gets on the sidewalk.

I think about pulling over and getting her number but decide against it. I have my hands full with Meechie. Besides that I really do like her a lot and want to give us a fair shot, so cheating is out of the question. I have wanted Meechie for years now. I can remember the first time that I saw her. It was about three years ago. She'd come with Shad to his daddy's cookout. Shad's daddy and my daddy are first cousins, which makes us second cousins. Me and some of my homeboys had stopped through. There were some bad chicks there but when she came none of them was messing with her. I liked her style and the way that she carried herself. She walked up in the spot like she knew she was the shit! She was mad cool too. She wasn't shy at all; she laughed and talked to everybody like she'd known us for years. I couldn't take my eyes off of her the entire night. From that day on I kept telling myself that I had to have her and whenever the opportunity presented it's self I was going to make her mine. A little over a month ago, I was out at the club with my boys and bumped into her. I bought her a drink and we chilled in the corner at a table most of the night talking. That's when I learned that she and Shad was no longer together. I confessed to her that I had been digging her for a while. We exchanged numbers before leaving the club.

After a few dates I was feeling her more than ever and decided to go ahead and cuff her. I definitely wasn't about to let her get away after all of those years of wanting her.

I go back over to Demetrius' crib and we go and make a drop. After we are done handling business I drop him off at his crib so that he can change clothes and I go back to my crib and change. The two of us meet back up at my crib and go to a club called Changez over on the eastside. When we get there we can tell from how packed the parking lot is that it's packed inside. We pay the twenty dollar admission fee at the door and then make our way inside. The DJ is playing some old school hip hop and the club is jumping. We go upstairs and pay five hundred dollars to get into the VIP section. We get us a table and our waitress comes over and takes our drink order. We order two bottles of Moet. We are chillin' getting fucked up when I look over and see Meechie, Carmen and their homegirl Nikki making their way through the crowd to a table with a group of niggas. I automatically feel my temperature start to rise! I get up from my table and go over to Meechie. I lean over and speak in her ear so that she can hear me over the music. "Who in the fuck is these niggas?"

"Excuse me? I thought that you had an attitude. At least that's the way that it seemed when you stormed out of the restaurant earlier!" She snaps rolling her eyes. "You said call you when I got my mind right. Well it ain't right yet, I'm still working on it so you can go on back wherever you were!"

She is really making me want to put my hands on her because of how simple she is acting right now. "Don't play games with me! I'm going to ask you again who these niggas are before I show my motherfuckin' ass!" I notice the cats at the table and Carmen and Nikki are now staring at me and Meechie but I don't give a fuck! They must be able to tell by my expression that shit is about to get ugly in a minute and they are absolutely right! If Meechie doesn't start talking fast I am going to give everybody in this motherfucka something to look at!

Meechie sucks her teeth. "I don't know any of these niggas! They are some of Nikki's friends that invited her here! She invited me and Carmen! Are you happy now?"

"Nah, I ain't motherfuckin happy! My girl is out at the club sitting with a table full of niggas wearing a short ass dress that barely covers her ass with her titties and shit hanging all out! Fuck no I ain't happy!" I'm heated and the alcohol that I have consumed isn't making it any better.

33

Meechie gets up from the table and storms off! I am right behind her! I follow her downstairs and out of the club. When we get outside she stops and turns around. "What in the hell are you following me for? You act like I did something wrong by coming out to enjoy myself! What you thought that I was going to be sitting up in the house crying because of how you showed your ass earlier at Lonnie's?" She sucked her teeth. "Nigga please! You got the game all fucked up, that ain't even how I roll! I don't need your ass like that...for real!"

I take a few steps back and look at her. "Oh really? You don't need me?"

"Nah, I sure don't!" She folds her arms and swivels her neck.

I let out a chuckle because I'm about to make her ass eat her words. "That's what's up then ma." I turn and go back inside still laughing.

Jada

I walk out of Black Beauty's hair salon looking like a different woman. It's been a while since I've had my hair straightened and it looks so nice. I am going to have to get it like this more often, judging on how the wind is blowing and the sky looks a storm must be on the way. I press the button on the remote that's on my keychain to unlock my car doors.

I am driving down Arlington Blvd on my way to the grocery store to pick up something for dinner. I turn on the radio and Elle Varner's voice fills the car. I turn it up some because Refill is my jam. I am singing along with the radio when the first drops of rain start to hit my windshield. I turn on my wipers. As I make a left on Fredrick St. singing to the music and hitting every high note with Elle I spot someone familiar walking down the street. I put on my signal and pull over alongside the curb. I turn down the music and roll down my window. "Hey, you need a ride?" I ask careful not to lean my head out of the window afraid that I will get my hair wet.

Shad stops and looks over at me. He looks relieved to see me. "Yeah."

"Come on." He jogs across the street and slides into the passenger seat. I pull from the curb back into traffic. For a brief second I think about what will happen if his crazy girl sees him in my car. I just saw her at the hair salon which means that she still might be in the area but I couldn't just see him walking in the rain and not stop. "What in the world are you doing out here in the rain?" I ask already knowing the answer to my own question, apparently doesn't have a car.

"Just getting off from work." He replies looking over at me. "I sure appreciate you stopping because it is about to pour down out here. I owe you one."

"You're good you don't owe me anything. You would've done the same for me...I hope." I glance over at him. He's looking like a chocolate God in the black wife beater that he's wearing showing off those muscular arms and shoulders of his. I feel a warm sensation in my thighs. I've always had it bad for Shad since we were in high school. I approached him once at a party back in the day but things turned ugly really quickly because it turned out that he was there with his girl Meechie. I've never understood what he sees in her. She's one of those loud project chicks that like to be seen. You hear her before you see her. She's very disrespectful and from what I can see she is one of those people who never mature. Today at the hair salon I overheard her talking about me to Chantel but I ignored her because to me she is not worth my time or energy. She is still walking around with a chip on her shoulder over something that happened years ago. I'll admit that I was wrong for stepping to her man like I did but I still feel the same way as I did back then about the fact that he can do better than her. I've always admired how much of a hardworking man Shad is. He has always been that way even in school. He had a job after school and instead of blowing his money on shoes and clothes he would help his mother take care of his sister and brother. I've never heard anything bad about him. When his friends and his brother were out getting in trouble he never participated in any of that nonsense. "Where do you live now?"

"In the projects over on Parker St."

"Okay, that's right on my way. I have to stop at the grocery store really quick though."

"That's cool. I can't tell you where to go this is your car." He laughs. "You are doing me a favor by giving me a ride so by all means handle your business. I'm good."

"I just saw your girl at the hair salon a few minutes ago. I hope there won't be any drama with me giving you a ride." I decide to mention this to him because I know that if Meechie sees us I will surely have to fight her ignorant ass.

"My girl...who?" He asks looking confused like he doesn't know who I am referring to.

"Meechie...duh. Why you trying to act like you don't know who I am talking about?" The rain starts coming down really hard and I turn my wipers up some. I look over at him waiting for an answer. Again I feel a warm sensation in my thighs and butterflies in my stomach. I feel like a little high school girl instead of a twenty-four year old woman.

"Oh we're not together anymore so you don't have anything to worry about."

I am shocked to hear that the two of them aren't together anymore but at the same time I am happy. *Finally he woke up and left her ass! It's about time!* "Dag I didn't know that y'all wasn't together anymore. That's crazy! The two of y'all have been together forever." I try to conceal my excitement, not sure if I am doing a good job of it.

Shad is looking out of the window. "Yeah well things happen. People grow apart...it's a part of life...I guess." He changes the subject. "So how have you been? I heard that you have your own café downtown now."

"Yes I do." I say proudly. "It's been open for a year now and business is going good. "

"That's what's up. Congratulations on your success!"

"Thank you. You should come by and check it out sometime."

"I may just do that."

I put my signal on and turn into Food Lion's parking lot. I find a parking space as close to the store as I can and park but the rain is coming down so hard I can barely see. "It's really pouring down out there and I am not about to get my hair wet! Do you mind if we sit here for a few minutes and wait until the rain let's up some."

"Nah not at all." He recline the seat back a little and get comfortable. "I didn't even know that it was supposed to rain today."

"Me either but I'm kind of glad that it did because it was hot as I don't know what earlier. We needed something to cool things off. Plus I love the rain…its good sleeping weather, especially if you stay in a house with a tin roof." I say turning the car off but leaving the radio on. I turn down the volume so that we can talk.

"Girl, what do you know about a house with a tin roof? You are too young to know anything about that!" He teases laughing.

I place my hand on my hip. "Excuse you? Ummm…first of all you are only like a year older than me so if I don't know anything about a house with a tin roof then you certainly don't!"

He playfully throws his hands up in surrender still laughing. "My bad…so tell me what you know about a tin roof then."

"My grandmother, on my mother's side, lived in an old house out in the country and she had a tin roof." I close my eyes reminiscing about how much fun I used to have at my grandmother's house. "Man I miss that woman so much. She passed a few years ago. We used to have so much fun together. I would go by there and stay with her for weeks at a time. We'd get in the kitchen together and cook up all kinds of delicious meals. She taught me how to bake some of everything, that was *our thing* cooking. We would go out on her porch in the evening and talk for hours. I would tell her about my dreams and goals. She would always say to me, "*Jada, baby you can do whatever it is that you want to do. You are a smart young woman and I see a lot of potential in you. I believe in you if nobody else does.*" That motivated me to go after my dreams even harder." I opened my eyes looking over at Shad. He was watching me attentively taking in everything that I was saying. "I hate that she never got to see my café. I named it Belle's after her. Sometimes when I'm there it's like I can feel her presence, like she's right there smiling at me letting me know that she approves because I went after my dream and succeeded."

"Damn...that's what's up." He looks at me incredulously and shakes his head but it's the look in his eyes that makes me feel a bit uncomfortable.

"What?" I ask shifting in my seat a little.

He shakes his head again before replying. "It's just that I never thought you were so...so...I don't know what the word is that I am looking for. I mean, I always thought that you were the bouji, high-maintenance type but you seem to be very laid back and down to earth. I guess that's why you shouldn't judge a book by its cover."

"Exactly. A lot of people think that about me because they don't know me but if they would stop assuming and take the time to get to know me. They would see that's not how I am at all." I let him know. "People look at me and say things like, *"Oh she thinks she's all that because she has long hair and a nice body."* That's their insecurities speaking because I have sense enough to know that looks can and will fade eventually. They also say, *"Yeah her family got money that's how she can afford that house that she lives in and that nice car that she drives."* It's true my family does have money but that's not my money. I'm not saying that my parents haven't helped me out along the way because they have and my grandmother left me a nice lump sum as well, which is what I used to purchase my café. As far as my car and my house, I bust my ass to make this car note every month and pay rent just like everybody else!" I shake my head as the things that I overheard Meechie saying earlier to Chantel replay in my head. "People should spend more time focusing on their own lives and trying to better themselves that way they wouldn't have so much time on their hands to hate on the next person because they see that they are doing better than them. They could do better too but they have to want it."

He nods his head in agreement. "You just said a mouthful! Damn I just got through saying the same thing to someone a week ago. People look at me and think that I am crazy or soft because I am not out here hustling chasing a fast come up. Shit, I know that fast money brings fast time. I ain't trying to go out like that, giving years of my life to the system that I can never get back." He looks straight ahead out the window, I'm not sure what he's looking at. "I have dreams too. I want to one day own my own shop. I love working on cars and fixing them up. I enjoy working with my hands. I have been saving up my money because this old dude on the eastside named Richard has a shop that he said he would sell to me for fifteen thousand. He said that if I can come up with ten. He will let me make payments until I pay him the rest. I'm not going to let anything get in the way of me getting that money. I've been putting in overtime all month. I am tired as hell by the time that I get home but I don't mind because I know that it will pay off in due time."

"That's what's up. If you continue with the mindset that you have you will definitely get that shop." I tell him smiling proud to hear a brother not only talk about what he wants but making moves in order to have it without turning to the streets to get it. After sitting here listening to him talk about his dream, I realize that we have a lot in common. I am very impressed by the determination that I hear in his voice and turned on at the same time. The rain has let up some and it is now only drizzling a little. I reach in the backseat and grab my umbrella that I keep back there for days like this. "Well I guess I will run on inside now that the rain has let up."

"Alright, I'll be right here when you get back."

"Come on and go inside with me." I am enjoying being in his presence so much that I hate to leave him for a second.

"Nah, I'm good." He declines.

I am a little disappointed but I understand because he did just get off from work and I am sure that he's tired. Plus when I picked him up he'd walked a good ways from where he works. "Okay well I'll be right back."

"Okay."

I get out of the car and rush inside the store. Inside I can barely concentrate on the things that I am supposed to be getting because I can't stop thinking about Shad. I can't stop thinking about our conversation or the fact that he is single. I blush just thinking about the possibility of us hooking up. It's funny how life works. After all this time that I've had a thing for him. Finally fate has stepped in and brought him into my life when I least expected it. I take a deep breath and exhale. *Lord, I believe that all things happen for a reason and I believe that it was no mistake that I happen to come through today when Shad was walking home. Please let me be right.* I think to myself before finishing up my shopping. When I get back to the car, Shad gets out and help me put my things in the car. "Thank you."

He looks at me. "Are you serious? Why are you thanking me?"

"Because it's the polite thing to say when someone helps you."

"Well you don't have to thank me. I would've looked like a lame sitting in your car watching you put these groceries inside after you were nice enough to give me a ride."

"Yeah...you're right...you would've." I teased. We both laughed.

I drop Shaud off and then go home and fix me something to eat. After I'm done eating, I wrap my hair up and take a hot bath. Later on I am lying in bed and all I can do is think about Shad. I wonder what he's doing. If he's asleep or if he's thought about me. I am too excited to fall asleep so I grab my cell and call up my friend ZyKia.

She picks up on the third ring. "Hello."

"Hey girl." I sing into the phone unable to conceal my excitement. "Girrrrl, today has been the best day ever!"

"Okay...what made today the best day ever?" She asks laughing.

"Well I was on my way back from the hair salon when I saw this guy that I went to school with walking. Before I go any further let me fill you in on the details, see I had it bad for him in school. I am talking baaaad! He was going with this girl named Meechie though. One time I got up the courage to tell him that I was feeling him at a party but he was there with her and she and I got into a fight!"

"Jada, you know you were dead wrong for stepping to dude when he was with his girl."

"Yeah, I know. Anyways so even after that I still liked this guy. Now back to today...it had started to rain when I saw him so I pulled over and offered him a ride. He accepted and got in. While we were talking he informed me that him and ol girl aren't together anymore! I wanted to jump up and down! Kia this might be my chance!"

"Maybe but don't go getting your hopes up too high. Just because he's not with her doesn't mean that he is interested in you." I take the phone from my ear and look at it. What the hell? I'm thinking that she is going to be happy for me instead she is over there bashing all of my hopes! "I'm not trying to sound mean or anything. I just don't want you getting your hopes up. Take your time and get to know him and see where his head is at...you know see if he is feeling you too and if he is then go for it!"

I think about what she is saying. She does have a point because I do have a knack for getting ahead of myself. "Yeah, you are right." I admit. "Well that's not all that happened today. As crazy as this may sound I saw his ex today as well, right before I saw him. She was at the hair salon. I am sitting there getting my hair done and I overhear this heifer talking smack about me to the girl who's doing her hair."

"Are you serious? How long ago did the fight between you and her take place?"

"Kia that mess happened like four years ago!"

"And she's still trippin' like that?" She asks. "How old is this girl?"

"Around my age but she is very immature as you can see."

"I know that you didn't stoop to her level and say anything to her, did you?"

"Girl no, I acted just like I didn't hear her. I mean if she doesn't like me that's fine. I don't like her either but I refuse to be petty whenever I see her.

There have been plenty of times that she's seen me and didn't say anything. I think that she was just showing off because she was around Chantel."

"Umph...that's sad. I hate chicks like that. I hope you know that if you and this guy hook up she is going to be a problem."

I'd been so excited that I never thought about that part. "Yeah you're probably right."

"If she is anything like you described, you know I'm right. I hope that you are prepared for the drama that is about to enter your life because ol girl isn't going to be happy about you dealing with her ex. She probably doesn't even want him but the fact that you and her have issues and she can't stand you over him anyways will cause her to act a donkey."

I sit up in my bed and prop two pillows against the headboard and lay back on them. "I don't see what would be the big deal if the two of them aren't together anymore."

"Jada the big deal is this girl is a drama queen obviously because she is still holding on to some mess that happened years ago! I'm not telling you to not deal with this guy. I am just telling you to be prepared." She warns. We continue to talk for a while before hanging up.

After hanging up I lay in bed staring up at the ceiling thinking about me and Kia's conversation. "Oh well, I'll deal with Meechie when the time comes! As for right now, I am on a mission and nothing and no one is going to stand in my way of having a chance to be with Shad. I deserve to be happy and live my life just like everybody else! Meechie don't run shit!"

Shad

I am up early the next morning cooking breakfast before I head out for work. My ma walks into the kitchen with her hair sticking straight up on her head, wearing a pink house dress with slippers to match and a Newport dangling between her lips.

"Morning baby, you sure have it smelling good in here." She says flopping her 120lb frame down in a chair at the small round wooden table sitting in the middle of the floor. She looks at me over her glasses. "You know that we need to pay something on the light bill before they turn the lights off. They sent a turn-off notice in the mail yesterday."

It was just like my mama to say good morning and then follow-up with '*I need some money!*' "I'll have something for you today when I get home. I will have to stop by the bank on my way home." I reply over my shoulder as I stir the grits. "How much is the whole bill? You know, to pay it off?"

"Shoot, more than we have." She takes a drag off of her cigarette before getting up and getting the ashtray off the counter along with an envelope. She sits back down at the table opening the envelope and taking out the bill inside. "It's $649.23 to pay the entire thing."

"What?" I nearly yell in disbelief. I've been giving her money every time that I get paid, never anything less than three hundred dollars! Her rent is only $475.00 a month; the water bill is never over sixty dollars, we don't have cable or internet or a house phone so I am confused as to why the electric bill is so far behind! She gets a disability check at the beginning of each month, child support for my little sister Tia and food stamps! "Ma, how did the bill get so far behind? It's too much money coming into this house for that. What are you doing with the money that I give you every two weeks?" I turn off the grits and take the sausage links out of the frying pan placing them on a plate and then turn off the stove.

"What the hell do you mean, what am I doing with the money that you give me? I pay bills with it! I buy stuff for the house! Tia needs stuff for school!" She explodes! "Shit three hundred dollars every two weeks ain't a whole lot of money! You act like you have been giving me so much!"

"In all I give you $600.00 a month! That is a lot of money! Too much for you to be telling me that the electric bill is overdue six hundred dollars!" I explain

51

trying not to raise my voice but it is hard because I know exactly where the money is going. She knows that I know and that is why she has an attitude.

"What exactly are you trying to say Shad? That I am blowing the money you give me?" She asks as I set three plates on the table. One of the plates I place in front of her.

"Tia, come on and eat girl before you be late for school!" I yell down the hall to my little sister who has been in the bathroom for well over forty-five minutes. Then I turn my attention back to the conversation that me and my mama are having while taking a seat so that I can eat. It's already passed 6:30 and I need to be out the door no later than seven so that I can get to the bus stop by 7:10. I have to be at work by 8:00. "I'm simply saying that there is no excuse for you to be receiving a disconnection notice in the mail."

She hits the table with her palm, accidently hitting her plate and spilling grits everywhere. "I know what you're thinking. You're thinking that I've been gambling with the money that you've been giving me!" She stands up and yells across the table! "Well I don't give a fuck what you think! Yeah, I play cards and go to bingo but that is after my bills are taken care of! The fact of the matter is you need to come up off of some more money if you are going to continue to stay here!"

For a minute, it was like I was experiencing déjà vu. She was sounding exactly like Meechie! "Ain't this about a bitch!" I explode unable to control myself any longer. She knows that she has a gambling problem but just like most people with a problem, she'll never admit it! She doesn't have to because it's plain as day! Shit, look at the argument that we are engaged in! "How can you stand there and threaten to kick me out, if I don't give you more money as much as I do for you? Aside from the $300 that I give you every two weeks, I help out around here by cooking and cleaning! I help Tia with her homework because you don't understand it and most of the time you aren't even home! Hell, before I moved back in I would come through and give you money to make sure that you were good! Now you have the nerve to stand here and say some foul shit like this to me?" I stand up to leave because my appetite is now gone! "It's really fucked up how everybody that I come in contact with is all about themselves!" Tia comes into the kitchen wearing way too much make up and a pair of jeans that look painted on. "Take your ass in the bathroom and scrub some of that shit off of your face! That ain't cute or attractive you look like a damn clown and I don't want to tell you what message that those tight ass jeans are sending!" I don't

53

mean to snap on Tia like I am but I am already heated and seeing her dressed like she's about to go walk the strip just makes it worse!

"Shad, why are you trippin'?" Tia whines giving me her best puppy dog eyes but that shit doesn't faze me one bit! I refuse to along her to walk out of the house looking like she does! I know how niggas be thinking. I would be thinking the same thing if I wasn't her brother and saw her step out dressed like a tramp!

"Girl!" I bark, warning her that now is not the time. She turns and stomps out of the kitchen back down the hallway to do what I've told her. She can see in my face and hear in my tone that I am not in the mood for any of her bullshit this morning!

"You need to check your tone in my house and watch what the hell you say out of your mouth when you are speaking to me." My ma starts back in on me! "You don't have to like what I said but I'm not going to change it! Either come up with some more money or find you somewhere else to go!"

I don't even respond to her. I just grab a few slices of bread from the bag on the counter; fix me two sausage sandwiches and leave. As I am walking up the street to the bus stop I wonder how much more of the constant bullshit I can take from people before I flip the fuck out! I am a good ass nigga who will do anything that I can to help the next person out but for some reason I am always getting shitted on! I'm not shocked at all by the foul shit that just came out of my mama's mouth because she has always been this way. I partially blame her for Shannon being locked up. She has always been money hungry as hell! No one could ever give her enough! A lot of the hustling and robbing niggas that he was doing was so that he could give her money! She tries to play everybody talking about the money is for the bills but shit it ain't like her ass is living in a mansion. She's living in a two bedroom apartment in the projects! I don't even have a bed to sleep in. I am sleeping in the living room on the sofa and she wants more money! I'm not giving her a dime more than I'm already giving her so I guess I need to start looking for a spot of my own! It's time that I get out on my own anyways. I'm twenty-five years old. I don't have any business being laid up on my mama's sofa. It was only supposed to be a temporary thing until Meechie and I could afford to find another place but then when we broke up and Mr. Richard told me that he would sell me his shop. I decided to stay and continue saving my money so that I can buy the shop. Getting my own place will cut into my savings and it will take even longer to save the money to buy the shop but fuck it! I've gotta do what I've gotta do.

By noon, I've decided that I need to start looking for a part time job. That is the only way I will be able to continue to save and get my own spot. I am thinking hard about my plans and where I can start looking for a job when my supervisor David calls my name. "Hey Shad, there's a beautiful young woman here looking for you!"

"For me?" I mumble. "Who in the world?" *Probably Meechie,* I think to myself. *Lord knows today ain't the day for her bullshit.* I leave the car that I am cleaning up and walk up to the front of the shop. I am surprised to see Jada standing next to David dressed in a pair of white capris, a pink tank top, with a pair of pink sandals. Her hair is down but the front is pulled away from her face up into a little pink bow. As I approach she looks at me and smile. I notice that she is holding a white bag in her hand.

"Hey...what in the world are you doing on this side of town?" I ask as the scent of her perfume invades my nostrils. It's a soft floral scent.

"Hey, I'm sorry for popping up at your job like this but you crossed my mind today and I decided to bring you some lunch. I remember you mentioning last night that you have been putting in a lot of hours so I wanted to do something nice for you." She holds out the bag and I notice the words Belle's Café written on it. "I hope you like chicken salad."

Damn, I am almost speechless. She has come all the way from downtown where she works just to bring me lunch. Out of five and a half years of being with Meechie, I can't remember her ever bringing me lunch. "I don't know what to say. This is really sweet of you, thanks Jada." I take the bag from her hand.

David clears his throat. "Ummm...why don't you go ahead and take your lunch break Shad. I'll tell Monte' or Devin to finish up the car that you were working on."

"Thanks man. I appreciate that." I look at Jada. "Come on we can go inside the break room where it's cool at."

I lead the way to the break room with her right behind me. We take a seat at the table and I take the food that she has brought out of the bag. When I open up the plate there is a huge chicken salad sandwich cut in two halves and lots of fries. "I can't eat all of this food by myself. Have you eaten already?"

"Nah, I'm going to eat when I get back." She replies.

"How about we both eat this?" I offer.

"No, I bought that for you. You could eat half now and half later." She declines but I refuse to take no for an answer.

"Actually, I had already brought something for lunch. So we can eat this and if I get hungry again I can eat what I brought."

"Okay." She looks at the table and then smacks her lips. "Dag I forgot to bring something to drink!"

I laugh because she is acting like it's the end of the world. "It's alright." I get up reaching into my pocket I pull out some change. "What kind of soda do you want?" I ask standing in front of the drink machine. "Your choices are Pepsi, Mountain Dew, grape, orange, Nestea, and water."

"I'll take orange."

I get her an orange soda and me a Pepsi. I sit back down and we begin to eat. "Thanks again for lunch. I really appreciate this. It's not often that anyone does anything nice for my black ass."

She looks at me with those beautiful grey eyes of hers. "Well maybe it's because your black ass is surrounding yourself with the wrong people!" She jokes but I can tell there is a little bit more to her statement. I've known for years that she's had a thing for me. She told me a few years ago at a party while Meechie and I were still together. Needless to say shit got ugly really fast. I'll never forget the whoopin' that Meechie put on Jada. I don't think she will either. Yesterday when she picked me up, I could tell by the way that she was looking at me that she still has a thing for me. I even peeped how she tried to pretend that she wasn't happy when I informed her that Meechie and I were no longer together. It's a good thing that she chose to open up a café instead of pursuing an acting career because she would be unemployed. I can't front she is fly as hell and I don't know any man in his right mind who wouldn't want to get with her. She's beautiful, smart, ambitious, and funny and from what I am seeing today very thoughtful but right now I am not ready to deal with another woman on a physical or emotional level. I still have feelings for Meechie and I don't want to bring anyone else into the picture until I know that I am completely over her.

I nod my head, chewing a mouthful of chicken salad. When I've swallowed all of the food out of my mouth, I respond. "You might be right."

"There's no might to it, I am right. You should never surround yourself with people who are selfish and always thinking of themselves. Those kind of people will only bring you down and completely drain you because you will find yourself always going out of your way to help them but when you need help they're never anywhere to be found! Also those types of people never come around unless they need something. You need people in your life who will treat you like you treat them, people who aren't around you just to get what they can out of you and people who will hold you down when you can't do it yourself."

The more she speaks the more I am impressed. I can tell that she is sincere about the things that she is saying because she is looking directly in my eyes as she speaks, wanting me to know that she is keeping it real with me right now. Also wanting me to know that, she's not just telling me to surround myself with just anybody but telling me that I should keep her around. "You've made some very valid points and I agree with you 100%. It's time that I start choosing the people that I let be a part of my life more carefully. That includes family."

"Hmmm...I know exactly what you mean. Sometimes you have to love family from a distance. They can be the worse ones to deal with sometimes."

I look at her sideways. "I don't know your family that well but from what I've seen and heard y'all seem to be really close and drama-free."

She burst out laughing flipping her hair back behind her shoulder. "Lord have mercy, boy you'd better stop listening to people and get your eyes checked as well. Haven't you ever heard that just because something looks a certain way doesn't mean that it's that way at all? Anything can look good when you are on the outside looking in!" She picks up a fry and takes a bite. "My dad's brother molested me from the time I was five up until I was eight years old. I remember when I told my parents about it, of course my dad tried to kill my uncle when he found out. I will never forget the words that his mother said to him when she found out though. We were seated in her living room and she told my father with me sitting right there, "She's lying because my son would never do anything like that! Her little fast ass has probably been letting those little white boys that live next door to y'all mess with her!" Uh..uh...uh her words cut me something deep! She made me feel like I'd done something wrong by telling on him or like I was nasty. It was already bad enough having to live with the things that he'd been doing to me but to hear my own grandmother sit in my face and say those awful things about me tore me up inside." Tears fell from her eyes and she quickly swiped them away. "People don't realize that when you are a victim of rape it's not physical scars that hurt the most but the emotional and psychological ones that hurt the most. You never really get over it because it's always there in the back of your mind." The more that she wipes her tears away they are replaced by new ones. "I say all of that to say this. I never stopped loving my dad's mother but

61

I never had much more respect for her after that. To this day I don't visit her, call, write, or anything. I love her from a distance. I can forgive but I can't forget. My parents have said that if I truly have forgiven her then I would have a relationship with her. They don't have to believe that I have forgiven her. I didn't do it because I had anything to prove to anyone. I did it for myself. It's just that I don't plan on ever giving her the opportunity to hurt me again. That is why I keep my distance."

I get up from my seat and sit beside her. I wrap my arms around her and give her a hug. I feel her arms go around me as well. "You are an amazing woman Ms. Jada. Not just amazing but strong. I am so sorry for what your uncle did to you." I whisper to her still embracing her.

"Thank you but you don't have anything to apologize for. You didn't do anything wrong, he did."

"You know, I see so much growth in you from the girl that approached me at that party a few years ago to now."

"Yeah because like you said I was a girl then, so I behaved like one. I've matured and become wiser over the years...I am a woman now."

"That you are." I smile at her. I release her and stand up. My break has been up but I was so wrapped up in our conversation that I hadn't noticed. "Well I wish that we could sit here and talk all day but I have to get back to work." She is wiping her eyes with a napkin now. "Are you okay?"

"Yeah, I'm good." She gives me a slight smile. After I clean up our trash, I walk her out to her car.

"Thanks again for lunch. I really appreciated it and enjoyed talking to you."

"I enjoyed talking to you as well."

There is an awkward silence as we both stand beside her car looking at each other. "Why don't you give me your number? I'd love to chop it up with you sometimes when you're not busy."

Her eyes light up and a wide smile cover her lips. "That sounds good, I'd like that a lot." She gets inside the car and searches around until she finds a piece of paper and a pen. She scribbles her number down and hands it to me. "Here you go."

"Alright, drive safely and I'll holla at you later."

"Alright."

Meechie

"Mmmm...hell yeah...go all the way down on that shit!" Rodney moans his hands are entangled in my hair pushing my head down further on his shaft. I open my mouth wider and relax my throat muscles so that I can take more of him down my throat. "Ahhh...shit! Damn that shit feels good baby." Gagging, I come up allowing him to slip from the mouth. I spit on it making it sloppy and then stroke him with my hand while giving his balls some attention. I take his sac into my mouth sucking gently teasing him with my tongue. I can tell by his heavy breathing and loud moans that he is enjoying what I am doing. I am topless on my knees on the floor in front of him and he is sitting on the brown suede loveseat in my living room with his pants down around his ankles.

After a week and a half, I finally broke down and called him earlier today because I saw that he wasn't going to call or text me. Plus my pockets were getting a little light and I am in need of a trip to the hair salon and the mall. Not to mention it's almost time to pay my half of the rent. If it wasn't for the fact that I need his money I would've definitely ignored his ass longer but to hell with the games my bills have to be paid! I see now that he's way more stubborn than me! I never went through anything like this with Shad. If we argued and he didn't hear from me in a day or two he would call and apologize just so that we could make up. Rodney is totally different. When I called him and asked why I hadn't heard from him, he simply replied "Because you said that you didn't need me." I asked him why did he have to take everything to heart. He replied, "Because you were the one trippin' when we last talked so I was giving you time to get your mind right! Besides, I knew that you would get it together and call sooner or later. You know that there isn't too many niggas in Jordan City that can do for you what I can. These lame ass niggas don't have the paper that I do! Your mouth may say that you don't need me but from the looks of shit your pockets are saying that you do!" He laughed arrogantly. His arrogance in some ways is a turn off but a turn on at the same time if that makes sense. I like how he thinks that he is running shit but at the same time I don't like how he thinks that everything has to be his way. It's all good though I'll let him run shit for right now...at least until he buys my car and puts me in a place of my own! I look at it like this; he's paying the cost to be the boss!

I am still sucking and licking his balls. "Put this motherfucker back in your mouth." He instructs. I do as I am told taking him back inside my mouth. "Yeah...that's it. Spit on it and make it real wet and sloppy. You know, I like that nasty shit! Show daddy how much you missed him!" His every wish is my command. I am working his dick overtime, putting down some of my top notch head game! "Mmmm...fuck...I'm about to cum! Gotdamnit!" He pulls out of my mouth and stands up! He's jacking his dick and looking down at me. "Can I shoot this shit all over your face?"

"Yes baby." I reply seductively while moving my hair back out of my face. I continue teasing his balls with my tongue.

"Tell me that you want this cum all over your face bitch!"

I am momentarily thrown off by the word 'bitch' but quickly dismiss it assuming that he is only caught up in the moment! "I want you to cum all over my face!" I am licking my lips and playing with my breasts. In only a few seconds he is releasing his warm semen all over my face. I rub my fingers over my face getting them wet with his semen before placing them in my mouth tasting his bitter fluid. "Mmmm...yummy."

"Ooooh...damn! Mmmm...baby get every drop of it!" He is shoving his dick in my mouth! I suck it until he is begging me to stop. He collapses on the loveseat and I get up off the floor. He sits there panting trying to catch his breath. "Damn baby you have some good ass head! Go and get a wet rag so that I can wipe my dick off." Without responding I go down the hall to the bathroom. First I wash my face and brush my teeth. Then I wet a washcloth and put a little soap on it before going back down the hall and cleaning him up. When I am done he pulls his pants back up and I take the washcloth back into the bathroom.

When I walk back into the living room Rodney is lying back on the sofa with the remote flipping through the channels. I pick up my bra and my shirt off of the floor and put them both back on. I am about to sit down beside him on the sofa but he stops me. "Before you sit down, look in the phonebook and get the number for New China and order us something to eat. I am hungry as shit!"

I go into the kitchen and look in the phonebook that is lying on the counter and find the number to New China. Walking back into the living room and picking my cell up from the coffee table I dial the number. While I am waiting for someone to answer, I ask. "Baby, what do you want to eat?"

"Order me some orange chicken with white rice, two shrimp egg rolls and a Pepsi."

"Hello, New China. How may I help you?" A female voice comes on the line.

"Hello, I would like to place an order please."

"Okay, go ahead."

"I'd like an order of orange chicken with white rice, two shrimp egg rolls and a Pepsi." I wait to see if she heard everything.

"Okay, will that be all ma'am?"

"No, I'd also like an order of sweet and sour shrimp with pork fried rice and a Mountain Dew."

She reads my order back to me and then asks will I be picking it up or if I would like for them to deliver it. I tell her I would like it delivered so she asks me for my address. I tell her my address only for her to inform me that they no longer deliver to the apartment complex where I live. I'm a little bit pissed that she's acting as if where I live is so bad that she can't send a damn delivery driver out here but I hold my tongue and tell her that I will come and pick it up. She tells me that my order will be ready in twenty minutes and then I hang up.

"You can drive my car to pick it up." Rodney says handing me the keys and a hundred dollar bill. "I want to see this movie. Stop by the store and get me a box of Newports while you're out. You can keep the change."

I smile taking the money and stuffing it inside the pocket of the little Apple Bottom shorts that I am wearing. "Thanks baby." I lean over to kiss him on the lips but he turns his head and I end up kissing him on the cheek instead. "What is that about?" I ask feeling some type of way about how he just played me.

He looks up at me with an agitated expression. "Because the only time that you want to kiss and all that shit is when I am putting some money in your hands!" He says matter-of-factly. "We good though, I'm chilling."

"Oh so what are you trying to say? You think I only want you for your paper?" I am standing over him with my hands on my hips.

"Nah, I'm not saying that you just did. I just take notice that you are most happy when I'm giving you money. It's really no big deal. Why can't you just go and get the food and let me watch this movie? We can kiss and whatever else you want to do later on after this goes off!"

"Whatever!" I wave him off ignoring the bullshit that he just said. "I need some money so that I can get my hair done tomorrow and you know that I have to pay Carmen my half of the rent this weekend."

He laughs while reaching back in his pocket, pulling out a wad of money. He peels off six crisp one hundred dollars bills and hand them to me. "That should be enough, shouldn't it?"

"Yeah, this is enough." I shove the money down in my pocket "What's so funny?"

"Nothing babygirl. Go ahead and get the food so that we can eat. If you hurry up you can watch the rest of this movie with me. It's really good so far."

"Yeah." I roll my eyes as I turn to go down the hall to my room and grab my pocketbook and then leave. Ten minutes later I am pulling into the Shell store parking lot. I have the windows down on Rodney's black 2012 5series BMW with chrome 24inch rims. The radio is blasting and I am bopping to 2Chainz. Everybody and their mama are up here chillin' at the store. I park so that everyone can see me. I check my hair and apply some lip gloss before stepping out of the car leaving the radio blasting and the windows down. I am a fly bitch who loves to be seen! I hear a few whistles and slick remarks from the fellas that are hanging out in front of the store. I don't even look their way. I act as if I don't hear them. None of them are worth my time. Half of them don't even have a damn job! Standing up here bumming change for cigarettes and beer! The last thing I need is another broke as nigga in my life!

I am about to walk inside the store when a guy name Omar stops me. "Damn Meechie, when did you cop that?"

"I just got it." I lie smiling and glancing back at the car. "You like it?"

"It's hot and you look hot in it." Omar replies licking his lips as his eyes roam up and down my 5ft. 3in. caramel frame. He is a tall slim brown skinned cat. He would look half way decent if he would get a haircut and a shave and buy some new gear. Tonight he is standing up here in front of the store with the rest of these bums, dressed in a pair of faded black sweats, a dingy wife beater, a pair of beat up old black Forces with a durag tied over his nappy ass hair.

"I know that's right." I reply. I am used to this kind of attention from men because everywhere I go there are men trying to holla at me. I'm not conceited or anything but I don't blame them at all. Most people say that I resemble the singer Brandy, I agree except for the fact that I am a little bit lighter than her. I am working with a nice little body too. I don't have a big ol' ghetto booty or anything but I do have a little bit of junk in my trunk and a set of perky B cups with a tiny waist.

"So when are you going to let me take you out and show you a nice time?"

"I don't know. You are going to have to let me check my schedule and get back to you on that." *How the fuck are you going to take me out when your broke ass don't have a car or a job? Nigga please!* I continue to smile at him, all the while I am laughing at his lame ass on the inside. When I decided to leave Shad, I promised myself that I would not fuck with anymore broke ass niggas!

"Check your schedule?" He gives me a funny look and then bursts into laughter like I've just told him a hilarious joke. The stench of his funky breath hits my nostrils and nearly makes me vomit! "Damn it's like that ma? What you got a nigga or something?"

I am about to reply when two girls come out of the store. One of them is short and a little bit on the chubby side. The other one is dark skinned and also chubby but she's tall. I overhear the light skinned one asks the other one. "Girl ain't that Rodney's car?"

"Sure damn is!" The taller one replies. "I don't see anybody in the car though." She turns and looks at me and Omar. "Did y'all see which way the guy that was driving that car went because he isn't inside the store?"

Omar answers. "Nah wasn't no dude driving that car, baby girl right here is driving it."

She looks at me with a shocked expression. I can see anger flash in her eyes. "Why are you driving my man's car?"

"Obviously there is some kind of mistake because that right there..." I point at Rodney's car. "...is my man's car."

"That is Rodney's car because the license plate says BALLIN' on it!" The light skinned one says as if someone has asked for her damn two cents!

"Okay and...your point is?" I ask with my hand on my hip and neck swiveling. I already sense that I am going to have to tear off in one of these bitches ass and that they are going to more than likely jump me but you best believe that when I get back home Rodney is next!

"And...my motherfucking point is...that you are driving my man's car and I want to know why?" The darker one takes a few steps advancing towards me. I also peep her friend getting closer as well.

Omar steps between them and me. "Y'all chill out!" He is trying to defuse the situation before it gets out of hand.

"Nah, I want to know why this bitch I driving my man's car!"

"Why the fuck you think? Because he gave me the keys! I mean bitch you look slow but you can't be that slow!" My adrenaline has started to pump and I am ready for whatever at this point! I've never been the type to run from a confrontation or allow any bitch to punk me and I ain't about to start tonight! "Now that you know why I am driving it, what is that going to change? Not a damn thing because I am going to drive it back where I got it from and there ain't shit that you or your big ass twin are going to do about it!"

"You want to bet bitch?" Rodney's so-called girl is screaming at me. She drops the bag that she'd brought out of the store onto the ground, spilling the contents all over the parking lot. "I bet you won't drive that black BMW away from here!"

Fuck these two whack ass bitches! I walk past Omar and them and head towards Rodney's car! I can show their asses better than I can tell them! No sooner than I get past them I feel somebody grab the back of my hair and pull me down to the ground. I fall backwards landing on my back on the hard concrete! As soon as I hit the ground Rodney's girl is on top of me! She is punching me in my head and face. I am doing the best that I can to block some of the blows! I can hear her friend screaming, "Let me go! I want to get a piece of that ass too! That bitch thinks she's bad!" Evidently someone is holding her! I turn my head to the left and spot an empty bottle lying next to me! From there it's a wrap! I grab the bottle and start swinging! It's not long before ol girl has to get up because I am wearing her ass out with the bottle that I have in my hand. I don't even care where the blows are landing! I just want this bitch to get up off of me! Once she gets up, I hurry to get on my feet! She is backing up and I am running towards her continuously swinging.

"Nah bitch, don't run!" I bark! "You weren't running at first!" My face and head are throbbing with pain and my left eye is swollen shut! My shirt is ripped and is barely hanging on. I don't care about none of that!

Someone grabs me. "Give me the bottle and leave! You know the cops will be up here in a few!" A male voice is saying to me. I am trying to push him off me but he has a firm grip. He snatches the bottle out of my hand. "Yo, calm the fuck down Meechie! Chill! Get your ass in the car and leave! This shit ain't worth you going to jail for, is it?" He is trying to reason with me but it's not making a difference. His words are only falling on deaf ears. I am seeing red and at this moment jail doesn't matter at all!

"Get off of me!" I scream still trying to push him off! I am using every bit of strength that I can muster but his hold on me is so tight that it's impossible for me to break free! Ol' girl is still running her mouth, talking shit! I can see that she has a busted lip but that isn't enough!

The person who's holding me turns me around so that I am facing him and I finally see that it's a guy named Reggie that used to hang with Shad. He grabs both of my arms and is shaking me. "Meechie let this shit go! You can deal with that bitch another time! Right now you need to get out of here!" Instead of waiting for a response he starts pushing me towards the car. I'm upset and crying, screaming all sorts of obscenities. He gets me to the car and forces me in on the passenger side. "Don't get your ass back out of this car!" He warns. Something in his tone tells me that I shouldn't try to get back out of this car, so I reluctantly stay put. He goes around to the driver side and gets in. We leave screeching tires headed towards the complex where I stay!

I am so upset and my head is hurting so bad that the pain is damn near unbearable! "I swear on everything I love that I am going to get that bitch!" I cry resting my head against the head rest. "I mean that!"

"All you need to do is calm the fuck down and leave that bullshit alone!" Reggie snaps.

"Fuck you!" I snap back at him! "Don't no bitch be putting her hands on DeMeechie Graham and get away with it! I might go to jail tonight but…"

He cuts me off. "Girl, hush that noise! You ain't going no damn where! Ain't nobody going to tell shit! You know better than that!"

"Yeah well…I still may go after I get home because I got something for Rodney's ass too! Who does that nigga think he's playing with?"

"Meechie, the best thing you can do is go home and put some ice on your face and let this shit go!" He warns as we turn into the complex where I live.

"Whatever!"

"Well, I got you home safely, the rest is on you." He pulls in front of my apartment, parking beside Carmen's car and turns off the ignition and hands me the keys. "Here you go."

We both get out of the car. "Thanks for bringing me home."

"No problem." He walks off across the parking lot and I go inside.

When I get inside Carmen and Rodney are sitting on the sofa watching TV and laughing. They both look up at the same time when I enter the room. Carmen is the first to jump up after seeing the condition that I am in. "Meechie what in the hell happened to you? Were you in an accident?" She comes towards me but I hold up my hand to stop her.

"Nah, I wasn't in an accident! I'm good Carmen." My eyes are fixed on Rodney.

"Where in the hell have you been? Did you get into a fight or something? Where is my food?" He sits looking at me waiting for answers and so I give him some!

Whop! Whop! Whop! I am swinging and connecting each time with his head and face. "Motherfucker here's your food! Does it taste good? Huh? You sorry motherfucker!"

Carmen tries to get between him and I. "Meechie calm, down! Chill out! What's going on?" One of the blows that are meant for Rodney catches Carmen in the side of her face. "Meechie, you need to chill the hell out! You are hitting me!"

"Move then! This doesn't have anything to do with you!" I tell her but stop swinging because my anger really isn't directed at her and I really didn't mean to hit her.

"It does have something to do with me!" She corrects me. "Have you forgotten that this is my place? I am not about to be getting put out over some bullshit! You need to calm down and talk about this like an adult! Not be fighting up in my spot, tearing up my things and shit! You are my girl and all but you are not using your head right now! Where are we going to stay if I get put out?"

"You're right this is your place...my bad." I want to tell her what she can do with her place but I can't because I don't have anywhere else to go at the moment!

"I didn't mean it like that Meechie. I'm just saying that I can't afford to get put out!"

"What the fuck is wrong with you?" Rodney asks. He is looking at me like I have lost my mind.

"You've got bitches attacking me because they see me driving your car! That's what's wrong with me! How come I didn't know anything about you having a girlfriend?"

"Because I don't have a girlfriend! That's why you didn't know anything about one!" He denies having a girl but I don't believe his ass! "What the fuck are you talking about?" He's looking all confused like he has no idea what so ever of what I am talking about!

"Oh you don't have a girl?" This nigga must think that I'm stupid!

"No!"

"Well why the fuck did two fat bitches just try to jump me up at the store? Some dark skinned out of shaped hoe claims that I was driving her man Rodney's car! This bitch knew your name and everything! When I go to get in the car she attacks me from behind! The only thing that kept the other one from jumping in it was that Omar was holding her back!" I run down the short version of the story to him. "Now you tell me why some girl would go through all of that over a man that isn't hers? No woman is just going to run up on the next chick claiming to be dealing with a dude that she isn't! C'mon now, you've got to come better than that? Do I look like Boo-Boo the Fool to you?"

Rodney rubs his hands over his bald head. "Baby...Meechie, I am telling you that I don't have a girlfriend but from the way you just described this chick. It sounds like you are talking about LaShaunda, this girl that I used to fuck with! She lives about a block away from the Shell store. I been stopped fucking with that bitch...probably more than eight months ago! I swear that bitch is lying!"

I stand there listening to his explanation not sure if he is being honest or lying to me. "So you mean to tell me that this chick is doing all of this and the two of you haven't been together in over eight months?"

"That's exactly what I am saying but I'm going to deal with her ass! I promise you that!" He assures me. "Baby, I would never put you in a situation like that!" He gets up from the sofa and walk towards me. Carmen moves out of the way but doesn't leave the room. I'm guessing that she's trying to make sure that everything is good. Rodney touches the side of my face. "I'm sorry. I promise you that I am going to handle this."

I move his hand from my face! "You'd better!" With that I leave him standing in the living room and go down the hallway to my room, slamming the door and locking it behind me!

Rodney

I follow Meechie down the hall to her room. I try to open the door but discover that it's locked. "Meechie open the door?"

"Leave me alone Rodney! I am not in the mood right now!" She yells from the other side of the door. "Instead of standing out there yelling through the door, you need to be dealing with that fat bitch of yours! I hope that she doesn't think this shit is over! Oh hell nah not by a long shot! I got that bitch when I see her! Now like you told me about Shad, I suggest you let her ass know!"

I'm not about to stand here and go back and forth with her. I can totally understand why she is mad; she has every right to be! "Alright, well I need my keys." I hear movement on the other side of the door and then a few seconds later the door opens up and Meechie sticks her arm out handing me the keys. "Can we talk?" I ask taking my keys from her hand. She doesn't respond just closes the door back in my face. I walk away from the door shaking my head. This is some bullshit! It seems like if it isn't one thing it's another. My relationship with Meechie has been like The Young and The Restless from day one! This incident right here isn't here fault though. I don't know what the hell is wrong with LaShaunda but I am about to find out!

I jump in my car and head over to LaShaunda's crib, when I get there she is standing outside in front of her house along with a few other people. I park my car alongside the curb and get out. I can hear them talking about the fight which confirms that it was indeed LaShaunda that Meechie got into it with. They are all boosting Shaunda's ego bragging about how she whooped Meechie's ass! I hear one nigga say. "If that bitch hadn't got her hands on that bottle you would've killed her ass out there in that parking lot!"

"That was the plan!" Shaunda replies bouncing around hyped. "She's one of those disrespectful type bitches that you have to show whose running shit!"

I can see that she is obviously feeling herself but I am about to deflate her ego and let her psycho ass know that she doesn't run a damn thing when it comes to Rodney! "Yo Shaunda, let me holla at you right quick!" I yell to her. Everyone turns and look in my direction, just noticing me.

"You are just the motherfucka! I wanted to see!" She yells walking towards the street where I am standing.

Her best friend Jamaica asks. "Girl is you good or do you need me?"

I answer before Shaunda can respond! "Yeah she good! Mind your fuckin' business!"

"Excuse you? Who do you think you are talking to?" Jamaica snaps.

"Your ass that's who!"

Shaunda is now standing in front of me. "Nigga who is the bitch that was driving your car at the store?" she demands to know.

"First of all you need to check your fuckin' tone! Secondly, this is my shit right here!" I point to my car! "Why the fuck are you worried about who's driving my shit! I don't fuck with you anymore! We been done!"

She gets up in my face! "We ain't done til I say we done! You ain't about to be with the next bitch I can guarantee that!" She says with conviction!

"What? Bitch you must be smoking some powerful shit! You need to take your crazy ass somewhere and get some help fast! How are you going to make somebody be with you! I done told you before that I don't want your ass!"

"Rodney, how are you going to say that after all that we have been through?" I see that she is getting emotional, her eyes are tearing up but that doesn't faze me at all! "I have been there for you when no one else was! When your mama was sick and about to die I was the bitch that was by your side!"

"Yeah and you were also the bitch that fucked my homeboy when I got locked up!" I remind her trifling ass while she's standing here trying to play like she has amnesia and doesn't know why I don't deal with her anymore!

"That was a mistake! I was drunk and it just happened! Don't stand here and try to act like you are all innocent because you're not! You fucked Jamaica!"

"Yeah I sure did but that was after what you did!"

"I forgave you though didn't I?"

"Shit it didn't matter to me whether you did or not! I was done with your ass by then anyways. That was some strictly payback type shit!"

"So what are you saying?"

"I'm saying, leave me the fuck alone and move on!"

She flips out and starts kicking my car. "Fuck you motherfucka!" she is yelling as she repeatedly kicks my car!

"Have you lost your gotdamn mind?" I roar seeing her kick my car like she's crazy! I grab her pulling her away she turns and starts swinging on me causing a scene! I am blocking her licks. "Go ahead now before I fuck you up!" I warn but she keeps swinging. I push her hard sending her flying backwards on her ass!

Her cousin Crawl, a tall muscular light skinned cat, which is known for fuckin' niggas up, runs out in the street where we are. Just as I turn around he punches me in the head dazing me. He continues to deliver punches to my face, I fall to the ground and he gets on top of me! I am trying to fight back but is no match for him. Finally someone drags him off of me. I can feel my face swelling and hear him yelling to whoever is holding him let him go.

I get up and stagger to my car, as I am opening the door to get in I yell back at Crawl. "Nigga this shit isn't over! Shaunda, bitch I got you too!"

"Let me go!" Crawl barks to the two cats that are holding him! "We can do it right now playboy!"

I get in my car and leave but this shit is a long ways from over!

Shad

A month has gone by and things are starting to look up a little bit for me. I got a part-time gig on the weekend working at Burger King. I am a janitor, cleaning up the dining area, taking out the trash and cleaning the rest rooms. It's not the best job in the world but it's a check! Fuck what people think, I'm doing what I have to do! I dipped into my saving and found a one bedroom apartment not too far from where my mama lives. The rent is four hundred dollars a month. I feel like I can handle that and plus my utilities and probably end up paying what I was giving my mama a month to stay at her crib. That's not bad at all and the best part is I don't have to worry about nobody putting me out!

I'm putting the last little bit of my clothes inside of a garbage bag and Tia is sitting on the sofa. "Man, I hate that you are moving Shad!" She whines giving me her best pout face. I can tell that she sincerely hates to see me leave.

"Awwww, you hate to see your big brother go!" I say playfully grabbing her up in a big bear hug and planting kisses all over her face! "I'm going to miss you too Lady Bug!" I call her by the nickname that I gave her years ago because of how red she would turn as a baby when she cried. We have different daddies and she has her daddy's complexion, she's a redbone.

"Get off of me! You are messing up my hair boy" She pushes me off, using her hands she tries to smooth her hair down. There are a million knots in her face. "Gosh, Shad you play too dag on much!"

"Girl be quiet! It's not like it's your hair!" I tease.

"Whatever! That's why your girl got stomped out up at the store a few weeks ago!"

Confused I look at her and ask. "My girl?"

"Meechie, who else?" She says like I should've already known who she was talking about. "Yep, I heard that some girl tore her ass out the frame because she was driving the girl's boyfriend car!" She's all hype now as she dishes the gossip about Meechie!

"Watch your mouth!" I warn. "Now who told you that?"

She shifts around a little bit and gets comfortable before running down the story to me. "Well the people that I heard talking about it weren't talking to me. I just over heard them talking about it. You know Devetra, Toya and Laura that live right across the street. They were up at the playground the other day talking about it. They said Meechie rolled up to the Shell store driving some dude's car. They say when his girl walked out the store and saw his car, she asked who was driving it and Meechie got smart. From there they say that girl went to Meechie's ass...I mean tail and walk the dog on her! They also said that Meechie picked up an empty bottle during the fight and hit the girl with it!"

All I can do is sit here and shake my head as listen to this bullshit that Meechie has gotten herself into. I never put her through any shit like that! It amazes me how some women will leave a good man to go and be with a man who puts them through hell! "Well that's her problem! If she likes it I love it!" I say getting up from the sofa so that I can finish packing my clothes. Jada is on her way over to pick me up to take me over to my new spot. She's volunteered to help me clean up and get things situated.

"I can't believe that I am hearing that from you!" Tia remarks. "I can remember when you would be ready to kill anybody who laid a hand on your precious Meechie, whether it was a woman or man!"

"Yeah well sometimes you have to learn to love someone enough to let them go. You'll understand that one day when you get older."

"Well that's not all that I overheard while I was up at the playground." Tia continued. "I also heard that even after ol' girl whooped Meechie's tail over dude, she still messing with him! As a matter of fact he bought her a car and they have a place over on Gretchen Avenue."

"That's good." Hearing that Meechie has moved in with Rodney bothers me some but there's nothing I can say about it. The two of us aren't together and so she has the right to do whatever it is that she wants! There's no use in me sitting around moping about it when she has clearly moved on.

Tia must've realized that what she just said affected me some because she says. "Well if you ask me you are better off without her. She never seemed like she was really for you anyways. All she ever did was act like you could never do enough for her but I never saw anything that she did for you besides give you a headache!"

"I appreciate that but I don't really feel like talking about Meechie anymore." I tell her.

"Okay." There is a soft knock at the door. Tia jumps up from the sofa. "I'll get it." She goes to the door and I hear Jada ask for me. "Yeah, he's here. Come on in." Tia and Jada come back into the living room. Tia is looking at me smiling like she just discovered a secret.

"What's good Lady?" I greet Jada.

"Hey you." She smiles. She's wearing a pair of grey stretch pants, a pink tank top that is very low cut in the back, exposing most of her back and a pair of pink and grey Air Maxx. Her hair is pulled up into a bun on top of her head.

"Tia this is my friend Jada and Jada this is my little sister Tia."

They both say. "Nice to meet you."

I look at Jada and laugh, shaking my head. "Women..."

She looks confused. "What?"

"New shoes to clean up in?"

She twists up her lips and waves me off. "Boy hush, I've worn these before so technically they aren't new."

"Oh wow, you've worn them one time!"

"Yep, besides just because I'm cleaning doesn't mean I can't look cute while doing it!" She says with a bit of sass like she's just made a great point.

Tia is laughing. "I like her! She's pretty Shad and she can dress."

"Thank you." Jada replies.

"Well come on Cuteness so that we can get some work done. It's already late." I worked at my part-time job earlier and didn't get off until two which is why we are getting such a late start.

"I'm ready whenever you are."

I tell Tia that I will see her later and to lock up the house because ma isn't there. I also tell her to call me if she needs anything. She assures me that she will and then Jada and I leave.

Jada and I are at my new place cleaning and listening to the radio. She is hanging curtains in the living room that she'd had at home and was nice enough to give me because if it were left up to me I would've just hung some sheets or something up to the windows and kept it moving. I am in the kitchen wiping down everything with Lysol spray. I hear Freddie Jackson's Tasty Love start to play on the radio. At the same time Jada and I both yell, "That's my jam!" My kitchen and living room are adjacent to each other. Jada turns up the radio and we are both singing.

I dance over to where she is in the living room, take the curtains that she is holding in her and lay them on one of the boxes that are on the floor. I take her hand and we start to dance all the while we both continue to sing. *"You work my love around and make it all come down. You give me that tasty love...oh yeah...ooo girl... you touch a special part of me a part that no one else has ever seen...ooo...girl...it's such a feeling that is so intense I have no defense..."* She stops singing and is just staring up at me as I continue to sing. *"Girl when you look at me. I can tell you see right through me cause I lose control of my heart and soul. Girl when you're next to me, the sensitivity inside you keeps me yearning..."* I continue singing to her until the song is over, she feels so good in my arms that I hate to let go but I do.

"Let me find out that you can blow." She blushes. "And what do you know about some Freddie Jackson?"

"The same thing as you, that he is the shit!" We both share a laugh and then get back to work, still singing along with every song that comes on the radio. A few times I glance over at Jada while she is working. Even though I still have strong feelings for Meechie, I realize that my feelings for Jada are starting to change. I have never been a slow nigga and I can see that she's a good woman. I

93

thought the same thing about Meechie at one point but with Jada it's different. I'm not just thinking that she is a good woman; she has shown me that she is. I still plan on taking my time but I know deep down that I'd be a fool to let a beautiful woman like her slip away.

A few hours later the apartment is looking and smelling good aside from the fact that I don't have any furniture. I have a TV that I bought from a pawn shop and a DVD player, both are sitting in the living room on the floor because I don't have a TV stand to sit them on. In my bedroom I only have an air mattress to sleep on but for the time being that's all I need. My stomach has started to growl. "I'm hungry as hell." I say rubbing my stomach.

"I've gotten a little hungry myself." Jada responds. She's sitting on the floor in the living room and has taken off her shoes.

"What do you have a taste for? I have a few dollars. We can go somewhere and get something." I offer.

"It doesn't matter to me as long as it's food. I am too hungry and too tired to be picky right now." Jada replies putting her shoes back on.

I stand there watching her and wondering what I can do to repay her for all that she has done for me. Whatever it is I know that it can't be expensive because a brother is on a budget right now. "How about some pizza?"

"That'll work." She holds out her hand and I take it helping her up off the floor. She grabs her pocketbook and put it on her shoulder. "You ready?"

"Yes ma'am." We leave out and I lock the door. Jada hands me the keys and tell me to drive. I take them and we get in the car and drive across town to Pizza Hut.

We are sitting in a booth enjoying a large Meatlover's. "Mmmm...this is so good or maybe I am just hungry." She says taking a bite of her pizza. She uses her hand to hide the food in her mouth when she speaks. "I don't need to be eating this pizza, all of this bread...calories. I have gotten too big as it is. I need to go on a diet."

She has to be playing because from what I see her body is just right. She has always been bad as fuck and over the years it's just gotten better. "A diet? Are you for real? For what?" I am looking at her with raised eyebrows.

She looks at me like I have lost my mind or something. "What do you mean for what?" She shrieks. "I have a gut and my ass is about to burst out of all of my pants and don't get me started on my hips. Ugggh...I have got to join a gym like asap!"

Shit, I could work you out! Better than Boflex! "You have a beautiful body. Do you know how many women in this world pay money to have curves like yours? You are blessed in all the right places and if you ask me, you don't need to lose a pound!"

She rolls her eyes up in her head and sucks her teeth. "Whatever, you are just saying that to make me feel good. You don't have to lie Shad, you can keep it one hundred with me."

I wipe my mouth with a napkin before tossing it onto my empty plate. "I would never lie to you. You already know that you bad so stop frontin'. I know for a fact that you have had a million men tell you so."

"Anyways..." She changes the subject. "I bet your sister is going to miss you."

"Yeah she told me earlier that she hates that I am moving but I've gotta do what I gotta do, you know."

"Yeah...I understands that. She seems like a really sweet young lady."

"Why because she thinks that you are pretty and can dress?" I tease.

"No silly...that just means that the child isn't blind and that she has good taste!" She teases right back.

"Sorry to burst your bubble but Tia is supposed to wear glasses and when she saw you today she wasn't wearing them sooooo..."

She squints her eyes and tries to give me an evil glare but it's not really working. "Sooooo...what are you trying to say?" She tosses a napkin at me.

I am laughing too hard to respond. When I finally get myself together, I say. "I'm just messing with you girl, you know that you are hotter than fish grease with your fine ass!"

"Hey Shad!" Someone says rather loud. I look up and see Carmen and her girl Nikki coming in our direction. They stop at our booth.

"What's up?" I greet them, not at all happy to see either of them. Carmen is cool but she's Meechie's best friend and so I already know that she only came over to be nosey because she saw me with Jada. Nikki is a straight up hoodrat that lives for drama. They are both staring Jada up and down.

"Hey Jada." Carmen speaks her voice dripping with sarcasm. "Girl, I haven't seen you in a minute. Where have you been hiding?" She asks as if she really cares.

"Yeah it has been a while since I last saw you as well. I haven't been hiding, I've been around. I just stay to myself and out of everybody else's business." Jada replies returning the same sarcasm.

"I know that's right girl." Nikki's phony ass chimes in. "I be trying to do the same thing girl."

Carmen turns her attention back to me. "When was the last time that you talked to my girl?"

"It's been awhile." I am wishing that they would carry their asses on about their business! I'm not the type to just disrespect women but these two are very close to getting cussed the fuck out because I know that they are trying to be funny. Carmen knows the history between Jada and Meechie so I already know that her nosey ass can't wait to go back and tell Meechie that she saw the two of us together. Honestly I really could care less what she goes back and tell.

"Well, you know that she has her own place now, don't you?"

"Nah, I didn't know. That's good for her." I respond nonchalantly. I know that she is trying to see if she will get a reaction out of me but it's really not that serious.

"Yeah, she's doing pretty good for herself. She got herself a new car too." She adds. "It's been a while since I've seen her so happy."

This bitch is really trying to be funny! I refuse to sit here and allow these rats to disrespect me as well as Jada. I don't like bullshit! "Well, like I said, that's good for her but Jada and I was trying to eat so if y'all don't mind we'd like to finish up our food before it gets cold."

"Hmph...damn excuse us!" Nikki replies laughing being all extra and animated. Carmen is laughing too. "Damn Carmen, I guess we'd better move along. People try to get brand new and shit when they get a new bitch!"

"Hold up! Who are you calling a bitch?" Jada jumps to her feet. Even though she can't fight, one thing is for sure she isn't scared at all!

"You are the only bitch in here so I'm obviously talking about you!" Nikki emphasizes. "Sitting up in here trying to be cute! I see your tramp ass couldn't wait for Meechie to get out of the way so that you could slide in! After the ass whooping that she put on your ass a few years back you would think that you wouldn't still be sniffing up behind Shad!"

I rush to get between them. "Jada, chill out. Don't stoop to their level!" I look at Nikki and Carmen. "You mean to tell me that y'all two don't have anything better to do than go around starting shit? From the time that y'all walked over here I knew that you were trying to be funny! I'm not with that petty shit! I am way too old for it!"

"You are the one who got smart because you are up in here with her sidity ass!" Carmen accuses.

"No, I told you that were trying to eat our food before it get cold!" I correct her. "Hell, it didn't take me to tell you that the two of you were being rude. You already knew that, like I said that was the whole point of y'all coming over here!"

"Hmph, don't flatter yourself boo-boo! You or this trick ain't that important to me on some real shit." Nikki says looking Jada up and down.

"I can't tell!" Jada shot back!

The manager, a short heavy set Caucasian man who looks to be in his late forties, walks over to see what all the commotion is about. Everybody in the restaurant is looking over in our direction. "Excuse me but I am going to have to ask you all to leave please or I will have to call the police and have them escort you all off of the premises. We cannot have this type of disturbance in here."

"All of that won't be necessary." Jada says throwing her pocketbook over her shoulder while giving both Carmen and Nikki nasty looks. "Come on Shad."

"Trifling bitch!" Nikki spats.

"I'll be that." Jada says calmly but I can tell by the expression on her face that she is ready to snap and I don't blame her at all. I feel bad that things have turned out this way because we were enjoying our night up until this point. The two of us go up to the register and I pay for our food and we leave.

The drive back to my apartment is quiet. When we pull up in front of my place, I park and turn off the ignition. "Jada, I apologize for that bullshit that happened at Pizza Hut."

Her arm is propped up on the door and she has her head resting against her hand. "You don't have any reason to apologize, you haven't done anything wrong. I knew when they walked over to our booth that they were trying to be funny. I don't care about those rats!"

"Yeah but I still feel bad. I don't like drama and I never want to bring any drama your way."

She looks at me. "Shad, that wasn't your fault. They are just immature as hell with no life! Right now they are on the phone filling Meechie in with all the details because that's what they do. They thought that little show that they put on was cute."

"That shit was a long ways from being cute."

"Yeah it was but they are too ignorant to realize that!"

I decide to change the subject. "Listen I wanted to tell you that I appreciate you helping me out. I was hoping that you would let me repay you by cooking for you next weekend. I know that ain't much but…"

"That sounds good to me." She says. "I would really like that but I helped you because I wanted to not because I was expecting something in return. I never know when I might need your help one day."

"That's what's up and if you ever need me, I got you."

"I'm going to hold you to that."

"Alright, so what do you want to eat next weekend?"

"I'm not sure. Whatever it is, I'd prefer that you bake it. I'm starting my diet this week so that means that I will be cutting out all fried food, bread, sweets and sodas."

"Oh lord..." I tease. "Damn would you just like for me to boil you a carrot?"

She starts to laugh and playfully smacks me on my arm. "No boy! Why are you trying to be funny?"

"The same reason that you are over there tripping about your weight. Haven't you ever heard the saying, if it ain't broke don't fix it?"

"Yes, I've heard that before."

"Alright then, so chill on all of that diet shit. You are beautiful just the way you are." I say sincerely.

"Thank you." She blushes. "You make it seem like I am over here downing myself. I love my body but I still would like to lose about 10lbs and get back into a size 11-12. I am wearing a size 13-14 now...that's a little too big for me."

"All I can say is a size 13-14 looks mighty damn good to me!"

She laughs. "Thanks silly."

"You're welcome but I am only speaking the truth." My cell phone starts to vibrate. I take it out of my pocket and look at the screen. Meechie's name is flashing on the screen. I hit ignore and turn off my ringer. I already know why she's calling and refuse to entertain any of her bullshit. She hasn't called me in over a month but no sooner than Carmen and Nikki run back and tell her that they've seen me with Jada, she wants to call. *Later for that shit!* I turn my attention back to Jada and we continue our conversation.

Meechie

I have called Shad's phone four times back to back but that black motherfucker is ignoring my calls! It's all good because when I see his ass I got something for him! I guess he's trying to be funny because he's with Jada's bouji ass! Carmen called me a little while ago and told me all about how he and Jada were booed up at Pizza Hut! I see that hoe couldn't wait to slide up in my spot! I guess he calls himself paying me back for fucking with Rodney by fucking with Jada! He knows that I can't stand that bitch! I see what time it is!

I walk into the kitchen of my new apartment that my boo Rodney got for me. It feels so good to finally have my own spot! Not only did he get me this apartment but he also bought me all new furniture. That's what I'm talking about...a real man. He also got my car, no more riding around in that beat up ass Camry! My baby put me in a 2010 midnight blue Nissan Maxima! I was planning on keeping the Camry because Shad gave it to me but now I don't want shit that reminds me of his ass! He can have that raggedy ass car and give it to that raggedy ass fake bouji bitch of his! I swear I am so heated right now after finding out about this Shad and Jada shit that if I saw him or her right now I would catch an assault charge! At first I was feeling a little bit guilty about messing with Rodney but now...it is what it is!

I open the refrigerator and grab my bottle of Moscato. I take down a glass from the cabinet and fill it to the rim. I need something to calm my nerves. I take a big gulp and think back to the other day when I'd seen Jada at the hair salon. "Trifling ass hoe, that's probably why her ass wouldn't look at me and kept trying to act like she was so wrapped up in the conversation that she was having with Felicia! She probably thought that I knew about her and Shad!" I say aloud. Even though I am trying my best not to think about the two of them I can't seem to shake the thought of the two of them together. "Whatever, they can have each other! I got a man, one that takes damn good care of me! Hmmm...I bet when Jada's ass find out how broke Shad is she won't want his ass no more! He trying to play me with a bitch that he can't even afford!" I laugh before downing the rest of my wine and pouring me another glass. After my second glass I am starting to fill the effects of the alcohol. *Fuck Shad!* I pick up my cell and call my boo. It rings once and then goes to voicemail. I press end and then dial him again. This time it rings several times before he picks up.

"What's good Lil' Mama?" He asks.

"Nothing much baby, I just miss you and was wondering if you were planning on coming through?"

"I am on my way to pick up some money right now and then I have a few other moves to make but when I am done handling this business I will be over there. How does that sound?"

"Sounds good to me."

"Alright then ma. I'll talk to you a little bit later. Keep it wet for me."

"Always." I say in my most seductive voice and blow him a kiss through the phone. He blows me one back and we hang up. I go and run me a hot bath and soak in the tub for thirty minutes. When I get out I put on a sexy black lace nightie and get in bed to wait for Rodney. Lying in bed I feel myself getting sleepy and before long I drift off to sleep. I am awakened a few hours later by Rodney shaking me gently.

"Wake up baby." He is planting on my neck. "Wake up Meechie."

"Mmmm...baby what time is it?" I ask stretching and yawning at the same time.

"It's a little bit after three in the morning." His hand is now rubbing my ass. "Wake up baby and give daddy some of that good." I can smell the stench of alcohol on his breath.

Wiping the sleep from my eyes I throw back the covers. "Hold on let me go to the bathroom."

"Alright, hurry up." He smacks me on my ass. "Damn...I am going to fuck the hell out of you, girl."

I go into the bathroom and empty my bladder before washing my face and brushing my teeth. When I am done, I go back into the bedroom. Rodney has gotten into bed and is lying under the covers waiting for me. I crawl into bed and he pulls me on top of him. He reaches up squeezing both of my breasts. I lift up my nightie and pull it over my head before tossing it on the floor. I lean down so that he can suck on my breasts and without hesitation he pushes them together and take both of my nipples into his mouth at the same time.

"Mmmm....baby that feels so good." I moan. I can feel my pussy become soaked. He is biting my nipples just the way I like. "Baby...hold on let me put it in." He stops what he is doing and I lift up enough so that I can put him inside of me. I slide down on his thick rod and began to rock back and forth slowly. He doesn't have a long dick but it is nice and thick.

"Ride that shit, ma." He instruct as he smacks my ass. I pick up my pace and began to bounce up and down on him. He continues to play with my nipples and it isn't long before I am cumming. He gives me a minute to get myself together before he tells me to turn around so that he can hit it from the back. After he busts his nut, we lie next to each other in silence for a few moments trying to catch our breath.

I am the first to speak. "Baby, why don't we go out of town and do something fun together. I mean, you are always busy handling business and I am always working as well. We don't get a chance to really spend any quality time together."

He pulls me closer to him. "Where do you want to go?"

A smile spreads across my lips. "Can I choose anywhere?"

"Yeah. Wherever you want to go."

"I want to go to Miami, Florida. I've never been so I figure it will be fun!"

"I've never been myself so we can do that." He replies shocking me because I thought that he would say no. "When are you talking about going?"

"How about next weekend? We could leave Friday and come back on Monday. Or maybe we could leave Thursday, so that we can have all day Friday, Saturday and Sunday to enjoy ourselves!" I am excited just thinking about how much fun I am going to have in Miami shopping and spending his money! After hearing the news about Shad and Jada, I definitely need to get away from Jordan City for a few days!

"Alright, that will give me time to make a few moves and make sure that everything is straight on the business end before I leave. I have to make sure that these niggas is on top of shit and that they don't be fucking up my paper while I'm gone. You feel me?" He asks.

"Yeah I feel you baby." I say reaching over to stroke his now limp penis. "I have something that I need to tell you."

"Mmmm...what's that?" He moans and I can feel his dick starting to come back to life.

"You might be upset."

"Meechie, stop playing...what is it?"

"I quit my job today."

"Why would I be upset about that? I mean, that doesn't take any money out of my pockets. That's on you."

Not liking how his response. I stop stroking his dick and I say, "Excuse you?"

"What?" He is now looking at me. "Why'd you stop what you were doing? That shit was feeling good."

"Forget that shit. I need to know that you got me...at least until I can find another job!"

"Yeah girl, you know I got you until you find something else! I told you that from day one. You're my girl you don't have to worry about anything! You just worry about looking fly and keeping your man happy and let me worry about everything else."

I smile and think to myself. *That's all I needed to hear baby! I am going to call first thing tomorrow morning and tell Walmart that they can kiss my ass! As for me finding another job...hmmmm not no time soon. I am going to lay back and enjoy being spoiled while this shit lasts!*

"I do want you to think some more about what I said about you going back to school though. That would be a good look for you. That way you will always have something to fall back on."

"Yeah, I am." I move the covers out of the way and take him inside my mouth. Later for all that going back to school shit there is money to be spent!

Rodney

It's the night before we leave to go to Miami and Demetrius and I are riding around taking care of some last minute business. We've just finished picking up money from the last spot and are on our way to get something to eat. Weezy is blasting from the speakers as we cruise through the streets blowing on some of the finest kush that Jordan City has to offer. Demetrius leans over and turns down the volume a little, "So when are you and Meechie coming back?"

"Monday, it's only a little weekend getaway. Meechie suggested that we go out of town so that we can spend a little quality time together. I agreed because it seems like when we are here there is always some shit popping off! Everyday it's something different!"

He nods his head. "I can dig it, son." Demetrius is a tall brown skinned, slim cat with wavy hair. Most would look at him and automatically assume that he is a pretty boy but he is the total opposite. We've boys for over ten years and I've seen this dude do a lot of grimy shit and vice versa. If I can't depend on anybody else to have my back out here, I know that I can depend on him. He's one of the realest niggas that I know, that's why he's mainly the only nigga that I deal with. "So what's the deal with Shad, he still trippin' off of you and Meechie?"

"To be honest, I really don't know and I really don't give a fuck! I don't see him like talking about it unless I take my car over to the spot where he works to have it detailed. Other than that I really don't see him. We don't run in the same circle, you know he's an ol' square ass motherfucka!" I laugh. "I told you about the last time I took my car over to the shop where he works he was acting like he had beef with me or something. The nigga didn't say shit but I could tell that he clearly had a problem."

"Well like you said he ain't say shit so it doesn't matter."

"True." We stop at the light and I am looking out the window. I notice that the car beside us is Crawl's black Nissan Maxima. We are driving Demetrius' Avalanche and the windows are tinted so I am not worried about him seeing me. He's chilling with the music turned up, I can see that he has a passenger with him but it's a chick. "Hey man, when the light changes instead of turning keep straight and follow this car right here beside us."

"Huh?" He looks confused and tries to see the car that is beside us. "Who are we following and why?"

"Crawl." I respond already feeling my adrenaline start to pump. I've been waiting to see this nigga again since what happened over at LaShaunda's crib! The light changes and just like instructed Demetrius follows Crawl's car. From the looks of things he headed home. We follow him for the next ten minutes and sure enough he turns in his driveway. Demetrius parks his truck the opposite side of the street. I am out of the truck and walking across the street before it comes to a complete stop. Crawl and his lady friend get out of the car and then she opens the back door and a little boy get out. "Yo Crawl, can I holla at you for a minute?" I ask as I walk up the driveway.

"Denise, go on in the house." He tells his girl. She doesn't move, she's looking at me nervously. "I said go on in the house and take lil man inside."

"Is everything okay?" She asks him but her eyes are fixed on me. I assume she can sense that I am not here for a friendly visit. By now I am standing next to the car face to face with Crawl.

"Take your ass in the house!" He barks at her but his eyes too are trained on me. She grabs the little boy and goes inside the house. "What's on your mind playboy?" He asks me. Instead of responding I swing, my first blow catches him in the mouth! I know better than to hit this nigga one time and stop so I follow up

115

with another blow, not sure where it lands. The two of us are going at it, he slams me against the car hard and then he slams me on the ground. He ends up falling with me landing on top. I am still swinging but my punches aren't fazing this nigga! He is fucking me up! Demetrius runs up and hits him in the back of the head! He falls over to the side and I get up. Once I get up me and Demetrius began kicking and stomping him until I see him start to cough up blood. I stop and tell Demetrius that it's time for us to roll out! We take off running leaving him lying in the driveway! As we are running across the street I hear his girl screaming and crying! I know that it won't be long before the police are on their way! We leave and Demetrius takes me to Meechie's crib and drops me off.

When I get in the house, I go directly to the bathroom. I turn on the light and look at the damage that has been done to my face. I have a busted lip, a knot on my forehead and the right side of my face is slightly swollen but other than that I am good. I wet a cloth and clean my face up. On my way out of the bathroom I meet Meechie in the hallway. My nerves are a little on edge so I jump. "Oh shit!"

"I thought that I'd heard you come in." She says and then takes a closer look at me. "What in the hell happened to you?"

"Nothing." I reply brushing past her. I run my hands over my face nervously knowing that Crawl's girl got a good look at me isn't setting too well with me right now because I know that the bitch has called the police. The good thing is I am more than sure that she doesn't know who I am and I'm not worried about Crawl saying anything. I know that I will have to deal with him again but I will worry about that when the time comes.

"Well nothing sure looks a lot like you were just in a fight!" She says following me into the bedroom. "What happened?"

"Nothing. Are you finished packing?" I ask trying to change the subject and looking around at the bags that she has packed sitting by the door.

"Yep!" A wide smile covers her face! "I am so excited! I can't wait until five o'clock gets here! I'm just going to sleep on the plane because I am way too excited to sleep now!"

"Did you go shopping for me like I asked you to?"

"I sure did!" She replies. "And I got you some fly shit too! I only bought you two outfits and two pairs of shoes because we are going to do some shopping when we get there anyways!"

"That's cool."

"So are you going to tell me what happened to your face? And why you have blood all over your clothes and shoes?" She continues to press.

"I already told you." I look down at my shirt and for the first time notice the blood that is on it, which isn't much. I assume that it probably came from my lip or when I punched Crawl in the mouth. I know where the blood came from on my shoes. I take off my shirt and shoes and take them into the kitchen and throw them in the trash. I go back in the bathroom and take a shower. When I am done, I dry off and wrap a towel around my waist before going back down the hall to the bedroom. I look in the top drawer and get out a pair of boxers. After putting them on, I sit on side of the bed and roll a blunt. As I am sitting there smoking, my mind wanders back to the events that transpired not too long ago at Crawl's house. I realize that me going over there and me and Demetrius stomping him out only made a bad situation worse but fuck it! I warned him that I would see him again. I didn't plan for shit to go down exactly the way that it did but it is what it is. I offer Meechie some of the blunt and she accepts. We sit and talk for a while and then I go to bed leaving her up.

We arrive in Miami the next day and from the time that we step foot off of the plane Meechie is going on and on about all of the shopping that she can't wait to do. All I want to do is sit my ass down somewhere. My entire body is sore from the fight that happened the night before. I feel like I've been hit by a truck! I don't want to spoil the trip for her though so I suck it up. We catch a cab to our hotel. The suite that we are in is absolutely breathtaking, I've never stayed anywhere like this in my whole life. The room is decorated in all white. There is a living room, kitchen, bathroom, one bedroom, a balcony, and a Jacuzzi. It's like a small apartment. The living room furniture is all white Italian leather, with a big ass plasma screen TV mounted up on the wall! The kitchen is decked out in all stainless steel appliances. I walk out on the balcony and love the view. We have a room overlooking the beach. There is ass everywhere! I go back inside and Meechie is running around like a big ass kid!

"Baby this shit right here is the bomb! Thank you so much for bringing me here! I've never been anywhere like this before! I can't wait to change my clothes and go out!" She wraps her arms around my neck and kisses me. "Come on baby and take a shower with me!" she is pulling me towards the bathroom.

"Damn girl calm down!" I tease. "You act like you ain't used to nothing!"

"Whatever!" she laughs looking back at me. It makes me feel good seeing how happy she is. We go and take a shower and then get dressed. We go to the main strip and get something eat and then shop until night fall. You would think that after all of the shopping and running around that we have been doing Meechie would be exhausted but she is ready to party so we change clothes again and head out to the clubs.

The next two days seem to go by in a blur because we are constantly doing something. I can't even front, I have really been enjoying myself with Meechie. This one on one time seems to have done us some good. It's Monday morning and we are getting ready to leave. I am just getting back from the gift shop because I wanted to get my mama a souvenir. She's called and reminded me a million times. I walk back into the room and as I am on my way inside the bedroom I can hear Meechie on the phone.

"Yeah girl, he has been spending money on me since we got here! Shit girl, I done hit the jackpot! Hmmm and he talking about me going back to school! I hate to disappoint him but I ain't thinking about no damn school! I am going to lay back in my nice ass crib, drive that fly ass whip he bought me and let that nigga continue to take care of me! He was the one who said that his woman deserves the best so I am going to sit on my ass and allow him to give it to me!" She laughs. "Girl, please I ain't looking for no job! I just told his ass that! What do I look like working when my man got all this money? I do work, I give that nigga pussy and head whenever he wants it and my shit is top-notch! Don't get me wrong it ain't all about the money because he is a good dude but to keep it one hundred, I ain't really ready for all of that falling in love shit! I gave that up when I left Shad. I just want to enjoy life and look good doing it!"

I am standing here listening to her and can't believe the bullshit that is coming out of her damn mouth! She's right, I did say that my woman deserves the best but I believe that she took that shit the wrong way! She's on the phone bragging to her girl like I'm some damn trick or something! Not only that but from what I am hearing she feels like I should be taking care of her simply because she is fucking me! Baby girl has the game fucked up but I'm not mad because I have something planned for her ass! She really has no idea who she is fucking with!

Meechie

Rodney and I are packing to head back to Jordan City after spending the weekend in Miami. The entire weekend has been like a dream! I've never had so much fun in my life! Rodney has given me any and everything that I asked for! I have shopped at Neiman Marcus, Bloomingdale's and Macy's! Those are places that I never imagined that I would shop! I've eaten at some of the finest restaurants that Miami has to off! He didn't spare any expense when it came to showing me a great time this weekend and making sure that he kept a smile on my face! There is no doubt in my mind that I made the right decision by dumping Shad and moving on with Rodney. I only have one life to live and I plan to live it to the fullest! Fuck being broke, worrying about how I am going to pay bills when I can be living like this and be treated like a queen!

We are on the plane heading home. I have my earphones in listening to my Ipod. I feel Rodney tap me on my thigh. I take my earphones out. "Huh?"

"Listen, I need you to do me a favor when we get back." He whispers to me.

"What is it baby?" I ask.

"I need you to deliver a package for me to somebody out in Marigold, VA." He explains. Marigold, VA is a little town about twenty minutes away from Jordan City. I guess he can read the shocked confused expression on my face and so he starts to explain. "I wouldn't ask you to do it but the guy that normally goes out there for me is out of town right now handling something else."

Did this nigga just ask me to deliver some dope for him? "Why can't you do it?" I ask with obvious attitude.

"I can't do it because I have something else that I have to handle when we get back. Like I said I wouldn't ask you to do it if I didn't have to. All you have to do is deliver the package that I give you and pick up the money. That's it."

"Nigga, have you lost your damn mind?" I snap raising my voice some. "What kind of bullshit is that for you to ask your girl?"

"Lower your fucking voice!" He mumbles through clenched teeth, his eyes are big looking like they may pop out of his head! "It's the kind of bullshit that I ask my girl, when her bills have to be paid, she has to eat, she wants to stay looking fly and wearing all of the latest name brand shit! If I don't get this money then you can't live this fabulous ass lifestyle that you want to live! You will have to end up taking your ass back to Walmart!" He shoots back! "Like I said if I didn't need you to do this then I wouldn't ask. Do you have any idea how much money I just spent taking your ass to Miami buying you any and everything that you asked for?"

I sit allowing his words to marinate before I respond. "What if I get stopped by the police on my way...then what?" I am not feeling this shit at all. I knew this weekend had been too damn good to be true.

"What?" He shakes his head. "Girl don't talk crazy. I wouldn't send you if I thought some shit like that would happen. Just drive the speed limit like you normally would and don't be doing no crazy shit to get stopped." He explains. "The money that you pick up when you deliver the package will be yours."

I take a deep breath and exhale. "Let me think about it. I'll let you know when we get home."

He leans over and kisses me on the lips. "Baby, I would never ask you to do anything that I thought would put you in danger or risk your freedom. Trust me everything will go smoothly. Besides like I said, I only need you to do it this one time."

"I'll let you know my answer when we get home." I repeat before putting my earphones back in and close my eyes but my mind is racing a mile a minute. All I can think about is if I do this and my black ass gets caught! On one hand my gut is telling me to tell his ass no but on the flipside of that I need him to take care of my ass so I can't just tell him no! I make up my mind that I will do it because he has been good to me and he is only asking me to do him this one favor, one time.

When we get home, I busy myself unpacking and hanging up the clothes that I got in Miami. Rodney has bought me a lot of clothes and I can't wait for these ratchet bitches out here in JC to see me in them! I know that they are going to be hating hard, even Nikki and Carmen! Rodney walks into the room and flops down on the bed.

"So what's up? Are you going to do it or not?" He asks tossing one of my little throw pillows up in the air and catching it.

I stop what I am doing and look over at him, placing my hand on my hip I take a deep breath before I began to speak. "I am going to do it but hear me and hear me good. This is a one-time thing and I mean just that!"

A smile forms on his lips. "That's what's up." He gets up off of the bed and comes over to where I am standing he puts his arms around me from behind and kisses me on the back of my neck. "You's a real ride or die, I see. I like that!"

I roll my eyes up in my head. *Ride or die my ass nigga! The only reason I am doing this shit is because it's benefiting me!* "Whatever." I reply removing his arms from around my waist. I am holding a Jay Godfrey maxi dress in my hand that I copped from Neiman Marcus that cost $460. I walk over to the closet and hang it up. *Yeah I'll make this run for you baby but if you think that you came up out of your pockets for this dress...then you ain't seen shit yet! I'm going to keep the money from the delivering the package and then some!*

The next evening I drive out to Marigold, VA to drop off a picnic basket to this old black guy that lives in this big ass house out in the country. I park my car in the driveway and grabbed the picnic basket out of the trunk and carry it up to the door. As I am walking up the driveway, I am looking around taking in the beautiful landscaping and how beautiful his home is. I can only imagine what the inside looks like. I ring the bell two times before the door of the beautiful country style home opens. Standing on the other side is a slim, tall, frail-looking dark man with grey hair. He is bald on top with hair on the side on his face is a full grey

126

beard matching the grey hair on his head. He is wearing a forest green silk smoking jacket, which puts me in mind of Hugh Hefner, a black pair of silk pajamas and a pair of black house slippers. The scent of his Polo cologne invades my nostrils. Around his neck is a thick solid gold herringbone chain. *Damn this old fucker looks like he is sitting on a lot of bread!* I think to myself.

He smiles at me revealing a perfect smile decorated with one gold tooth. "Hello there and how may I help you?" He asks politely in his heavy southern accent.

I smile back nervously. All I want to do is give him this basket of shit, get my money and dip! "Ummmm...I'm looking for Douglas."

"I am him, come in please." He steps back to let me in. I walk in and stand beside the door. Just as I'd figured his house is decked out inside, like some shit that you would see in a magazine or on TV. I believe that my mouth is hanging open as I take in all of the artwork hanging on the walls, the beautiful statues, the winding staircase, etc. I instantly fall in love with his home! This is the way that I want to live and I will some day! "Do you like what you see?" he asks.

"Yes sir, your home is absolutely gorgeous!"

127

"Thank you but it's nothing compared to your beauty." He winks openly flirting with me.

I smile politely and thank him for the compliment before handing him the basket. "This is for you."

He takes the basket and sits it down and then reaches inside the pocket of his smoking jacket and pull out an envelope. "And this is for you."

I take the envelope from his hand and stuff it inside my handbag. "Thank you and it was nice meeting you." I say and turn to leave.

"Hold on beautiful. I didn't get your name." He touches my arm.

I know good and damn well his old ass ain't trying to get fresh with me! "I'm Meechie."

"It's nice to meet you, Meechie. Can I ask you something?"

"Sure." I reply hoping that he is not about to ask me for some ass or something crazy. I don't know, he could be an old freak or something!

"What in the world is a beautiful young woman like yourself doing delivering dope?"

Instead of answering his question, I decide to ask one of my own. "What is an old man like yourself doing smoking dope?"

He throws his head back and laugh clapping his hands together. "Beautiful, I ain't smoking this shit! If you must know I throw a lot of parties and a lot of my guests like to get high so I make sure that I have what they like. Now answer my question."

I drop my head kind of embarrass, not really sure why. "My boyfriend needed me to deliver this for him because he was in a bind and didn't have anyone else who could do it."

He takes his hand and lift up my head. "He isn't a real man and he doesn't give damn about you because if he did he would never have asked you to do this."

Even though I felt the same way when Rodney had asked me to do this for some reason I am offended hearing him speak about my relationship like he knows what Rodney feels for me! "Excuse me, how do you know whether or not he cares for me? For your information he does give a damn about me because he takes damn good care of me and I don't want for nothing!" I turn and open the door and storm out! I can hear him laughing from behind me so I stop and turn around. "May I ask what the fuck is so gotdamn funny? Your old ass must be high or something because I don't see shit funny!" I yell at him.

He walks down off the porch and stops in front of me. "I am laughing at how blind you young women are! You are quick to fly off at the mouth, that's your biggest problem! Instead of running your mouth, keep it closed and open your eyes. You might just see that he ain't giving you shit! Your ass is working for whatever it is that *your man* is giving you! Why do you think that you are here delivering *your man's* dope to me?"

I swear this motherfucka don't know when to quit! "Ummm if you turn up your damn hearing aid you would have heard me say that he was in a bind! This is the first time that he's ever asked me to do this for him!"

"I bet it won't be the last!" He turns and starts walking back towards the house. "I'll see you soon, Beautiful! When you decide you are ready for a real man, come and holla at my *old ass!*" He is still laughing. "I can show you how a real man is supposed to treat a beautiful woman like yourself and you won't have to worry about delivering dope anymore!"

"Fuck you!" I yell and jump in my car and leave. On the way back to JC all I can think about is how old dude was all up in my business trying to play me! I contemplate whether or not I should tell Rodney about what just happen but then decide against it. I figure to myself that dude was probably high and just running of at the mouth! Fuck him and his opinion!

When I get home I call Rodney and let him know that everything went smoothly and that I made it back safely. "That's what's up ma. I told you that everything would be alright." He says. "Listen I am handling some business right now so I am going to hit you up a little later."

"Alright." We hang up and I walk over and stand looking out of my living room window. Though things are pretty good right now and I have everything that I wanted I still feel like something is missing. My eyes fall on the Camry that Shad gave me parked next to the car that Rodney gave me. I think back to the day that he gave me that ugly ass car and I can't help but smile.

He was so excited that day when he came over to my apartment. I was lying on the sofa taking a nap. I'd just worked a double shift at Walmart and then had to walk home from the bus stop. My feet were killing me. Loud banging on the door jolted me from my sleep. I sat up on the sofa and looked around still half asleep. The banging started again. I got up from the sofa stumbling over my sneakers that I'd taken off before going to sleep. "Shit!" I cursed. The person on the other side of the door banged again! "I'm coming damn it!" I yelled. When I reached the door I snatched it open, my face twisted in a million knots!

Shad was standing there smiling. "Damn girl, you were in a coma weren't you?" He joked.

"No, I was sleep shit! Why in the hell are you banging on the damn door like that?" I griped!

"Hush, that noise." He replied ignoring my attitude. "I have a surprise for you. Come downstairs o you can see it!"

I turned and stomped back over to the sofa leaving the door opened for him. I flopped down and laid my head on the arm of the sofa. "Shad whatever it is it can wait! I am tired as hell and my feet are killing me. You know that I worked a double today and then had to walk all the way from the bus stop! This walking shit is in the way! Standing at the bus stop waiting on the bus and shit! I need a damn car!" I went on and on complaining.

When I was done he simply asked. "Are you done?" I rolled my eyes feeling as though he was ignoring everything that I'd just said. "Slip on your shoes and come downstairs real quick."

"Shad, what part of I'm tired don't you understand?"

"Girl, shut up and bring your ass on here." He snapped looking agitated. "You ruin everything with all of that damn whining and complaining! Damn!"

I slipped my feet back in my sneakers and got up from the sofa. He lead the way outside with me right behind him. When we got down to the parking lot he stopped beside a red beat up Camry. He reached in his pocket and took out a set of keys and handed them to me. "What are these for?" I asked taking the keys from him wearing a confused expression.

"They're yours so that you can start your car!"

"My car?"

"Yep." He smiled proudly and pointed to the Camry. "I bought it from my homeboy Dre for you. I know that it isn't much but at least now you won't have to be catching rides, walking or standing at the bus stop."

Even though I wasn't crazy about the appearance of the ugly ass car, I was happy as hell not to be walking any longer! I smile at the memory but my smile quickly turns into a frown when I think about Shad's new relationship with Jada. I just can't get over that shit! Out of all people, why her? I take my cell out of my pocket and dial Carmen's number, it rings several times but she doesn't answer and it goes to voicemail. I hang up and dial Nikki next. She picks up after two rings.

"What up chic?" She asks.

"Hey girl, are you busy?"

"Nah, what's up? I'm just over here bullshitting with Dreka and Val.

"Can you meet me over at the detailing shop over on Skeeter Blvd. where Shad works? I am about to drop the Camry off over there and I am going to need a ride back home. I'll give you a few dollars for gas."

I hear her smack her lips. "Chic don't even try and play me talking about you gone pay be for some gas! You know that you are good, I'll be there when you get there boo."

"Alright." I hang up and grab the keys to the car, my house keys, and my pocketbook and then leave. When I get to the shop Nikki is already there waiting on me. I park the car and tell her that I will be right back. As I am about to open the door to go inside Shad is coming out. He looks surprised to see me.

"Hey, what are you doing here?" He asks.

I hold up the keys. "Returning your car."

"Returning my car? I bought that car for you."

"Well I have a new one now and no longer need it!" I smirk. "Give it to your bitch!"

"Really? Are you really that fucking immature?" He takes the keys from my hand. "You know, what I ain't even going to go there with you today. It's been a long day and I'm tired and I still have to go to my other job so it is what it is."

Hearing him mention that he now has a second job pisses me off! "What you can go and get another job now since you are with that bitch but when I was complaining about us not having enough money to make ends meet you couldn't do that!"

"Meechie, bye. I don't have time for your bullshit!"

I get in his face. "So what are you trying to say that she is worth more than me?"

"Will you listen at yourself?" He asks. "Does that shit even make sense? I got another job because I moved out of my mama's spot and in order for me to still save to buy the shop and get my own place I had to!"

This was my first time learning that he had his own place which further infuriated me! "I begged your black ass for months to let's get our own place but you claimed like we couldn't afford it!"

"We couldn't afford the places that you wanted! You wanted to live out there in the fancy ass white folks neighborhood! You wanted an apartment with over eight hundred dollar rent! At the same time you wanted to spend your entire paycheck at the mall on them lil slutty ass outfits, getting your nails and hair done and buying shoes and shit! I told you, you want a whole lot of shit Meechie but you don't want to sacrifice shit for it or work for it! To keep it real you want a free fucking ride just like most motherfuckas but remember ain't shit free! In one way or another you're paying for it!"

I'm not trying to hear this bullshit that he is saying. "You know what, leaving your ass was the best move that I've ever made! Now I have the nice place that I've always wanted with brand new furniture throughout the entire place, I'm driving a 2011 Nissan Maxima, and I stays fly! I've been quit that raggedy ass job at Walmart! I have a real man now, one who doesn't bitch and complain about what he can't do or what he can't afford. He gets out and makes shit happen! As a matter of fact we just got back from Miami!"

He stands here looking unaffected but I know that my words have hit a nerve whether he shows it or not. "As long as you're happy, I'm happy. Now if you don't mind, I have to go to work. I appreciate you bringing the car though so now I don't have to walk out here in this hot ass sun to the bus stop." He lets out a chuckle. "I might couldn't afford a 2011 Nissan Maxima but this beat up ass Camry kept your ungrateful ass from walking a many of days! I get it though, Meechie. You want the finest things that money can buy. Ain't nothing wrong with that babygirl...nothing at all. Just remember that the best things in life are priceless."

I roll my eyes. "Whatever!"

"You have a good day now."

"Trust me, I will!" I say with much attitude! He walks over to the Camry and gets in and drives off.

Jada

Two months have flown by and things between Shad and I have changed a lot. We have gotten extremely close. Whenever he's not working and I'm not, we are together. My feelings for him have grown tremendously; just the mention of his name has me blushing for hours. I can without a doubt say that I am so in love with him. I'm not exactly why he and Meechie broke up and to be honest I don't care. I'm just glad that they did. The two of us have so much fun together. We don't even have to be out doing anything. We can stay in and talk for hours, watching movies, and of course debating about everything and it's the best time in the world! We just click. I can tell that his feelings for me have grown a lot as well. I can see it in his eyes when he looks at me or how we can just be sitting on the floor in his living room watching TV and he'll reach over and take my hand. Uuuuggghhh... I have fallen so hard for this man! As the old folks say, he has my nose wide open! I've never had anyone who makes me feel the way that he does.

I am at work sweeping up and humming along to a Nina Simone record that is playing. There are a few customers here, eating and some quietly reading. I love my café and the relaxed vibe that I feel when I am here. I am deep in thought thinking about the book signing that will be held here this weekend. I'm very excited because the author is a local author who just released his first book that he self-published on his own. He came in a few weeks ago and asked me if he could host his first book signing and discussion here. I was very flattered that he'd asked to do it here and agreed to let him. He even gave me an autographed copy, a few extra copies to pass out to my customers, flyers and bookmarks as well. I read the book and loved it and the people that I gave the extra copies to all informed me that they loved it too and can't wait until this weekend to discuss the book with him. I am just glad that I could help.

My train of thought is interrupted when, ZyKia, walks over to where I am sweeping. She's been here since I opened a year ago and in that time we have become pretty close. "Girrrrl..." She sings the word. "What's up with you and Shad? You've been all hush mouth! Come on and dish the gossip chile!" She is grinning like a Chester Cheeto waiting and anticipating some info! She has her hand on her thick hip. ZyKia is a big girl weighing somewhere around 290 to 300lbs but she wears it well and is always dressed to impressed with her makeup done to perfection. She's one of those big girls who is comfortable in her skin and feels that she's beautiful just the way that she is. She wears her hair cut in a chin length auburn bob with honey blonde highlights that that frames her round face and compliments her mahogany brown skin.

I blush at the mention of Shads name. "There's nothing to tell. We are just friends."

"Mmmmmhmmm...yeah for now!" She teases. "Don't play with me heifer! You have told me how you feel about this guy so you can stop all of that we are just friends crap! Every time that I turn around you two is on the phone or you are somewhere sitting in a corner texting him! I got a peek at him the other day when he stopped by here to see you. He is fine as shit girl! I love me some chocolate men! You're lucky that I was busy when he came in here because if I hadn't been I would've been trying to steal his lil fine ass from you!" She teases.

"Girl, hush your mouth!" I laugh at my silly friend. "As for Shad and I texting and calling each other all the time, friends text and call each other." I sweep my trash into the dust pan and then dump it in the trash. When I am done I take a seat at one of the tables and ZyKia joins me.

"That is true but it's been about four months now since the two of you started talking. You mean to tell me that y'all haven't even kissed?"

The big smile on my face answers her question. "Yes, we have...the other night when I went over to his place. He cooked dinner for me and then we watched a movie. When I was leaving he walked me out to my car. I was looking for him to hug me like he normally does but honeyyyy..." I throw my hands up in the air like I am about to testify to the good Lord! "Girl, that man laid a kiss on me that made me weak in the knees and crossed eyed all at the same time. ZyKia, I nearly had an orgasm standing right there in the parking lot!"

"Damn!" She laughed. "Shad ain't no joke is he?"

"Hmmmm...Zy, I am so gone over this man. I am in love." I look at her in the eyes and admit truthfully.

"Wow, well how does he feel about you? I mean, what about his ex? Is he completely over her? You don't want to get caught up being his rebound."

"Well, I can't sit here and tell you that he is completely over her because you can't love someone one day and not the next. Love doesn't work that way. I do believe that he has realized that it's time to move forward." I answer. "When he looks at me there is a strong connection between us. I can tell by the way that he when we are together that his feelings for me have grown. I am not trying to rush him into anything. I want whatever he is feeling or is going to feel towards me to develop naturally. That way I will know that it is real."

"I agree, y'all don't need to rush into anything because if you do it won't turn out good." She replies. "I just want to see you happy Jada. You are my friend and I love you to death. I've sat and listen to you tell me about all of the things that you have been through and after hearing all of that I want happiness for you more than anything. I don't want to see you get hurt by Shad and so I hope that he knows what he wants."

"Yeah me too." I sit there and think a minute before revealing to her what has been eating at me for the past few weeks. "I wonder how Shad will react when he finds out that I am sterile."

Zy looks at me sympathetically and reaches across the table and squeeze my hand lightly. "If he is this great man that you make him out to be, he will understand and accept you just as you are the same way that you have accepted him, flaws and all. What happened to you wasn't your fault. I swear every time that I think about what your sorry as uncle did to you. I get mad all over again! They should've given his ass life in prison instead of fifteen years. Fifteen years isn't enough time for what he took from you and what he put you through. You will never completely heal from what he did to you."

"I know...I just wish that I had told my parents sooner. That way the STD that he gave me could've been treated sooner and I wouldn't have been left unable to have kids. I've went to a few different doctor and they all say it would be impossible for me to conceive."

"There is always adoption."

"Yeah but..." There is laughter at the door. I look up and see two women walking in. I stand to greet them. "Good afternoon, welcome to..." My words get stuck in my throat when I see that the women are Meechie and Carmen. *Lord not today!* I think to myself. Meechie has been picking for months now. Whenever she sees me she makes little slick comments loud enough for me to hear her. This chic really needs to quit! Now she has the audacity to come walking up in my café'! I'm not sure how much longer I can try to be the bigger woman and continue to ignore her bullshit!

"What's wrong Jada?" Zy asks obviously noticing the look on my face.

"Nothing." I plaster a fake smile on my face and try to remember that I am at my place of business and it is important for me to remain professional. "Hello ladies."

"Hey." Carmen speaks. "We were in the area and figured we would stop in for a bite to eat."

"Alright, well you can have a seat anywhere that you'd like." I say. "Let me go and grab you two some menus."

They take a seat at one of the tables and I can hear them giggling. I go over behind the counter and get them two menus and silverware. I carry everything to their table and place it in front of them. "What can I get you to drink?" I ask.

"Ummmm...let me see." Meechie says looking over the menu. "I'll have the mint green tea sweetened with honey."

"I'll just take a sweet tea with lots of ice." Carmen replies.

"Alright. I'll be right back with your drinks." I leave their table and go to fix their drinks.

Zy is now back in the kitchen area. "Do you know them?"

"Yes, that's Shad's ex Meechie and her friend Carmen."

"Carmen…Carmen…" She repeats. "Don't I remember you telling me something about having some words with a girl named Carmen at Pizza Hut a little while back?"

"Yeah, her and another girl were at Pizza Hut. They came over to me and Shad's table trying to be funny."

"Oh hell nah, so let me guess…they came in here trying to be funny as well?"

"Pretty much." I reply grabbing the two drinks I've just fixed to take back out to Meechie and Carmen.

"Well I'll tell you what, they had better be on their best behavior today or I'm going to set it off in here! I don't like immature little girls that go around picking at people who aren't even thinking about them!"

"Me either but hopefully they will eat their food and leave. I know they are just coming to be nosey and be funny but I am not going to stoop to their level. I am going to remain professional because this is my place of business and I refuse to let my customers see me in here acting a donkey!"

Zy rolls her eyes and smacks her lips. "Okay Ms. Professional but if them heifers get out of line you had better put them in their place. Don't allow them little girls to come up in here disrespecting you because if you let them do it now then they will continue every time that they see you." She warns.

"I know." I leave Zy standing in the kitchen and take Meechie and Carmen their drinks. "Here you are ladies." I say as I sit their drinks down in front of them. "Is there anything else that I can get for you?"

"Yes, I would like the turkey wrap with ranch dressing." Carmen says.

"I'll have the same." Meechie says looking me up and down. "I am trying to watch my weight. I don't want to get all fat and sloppy...you know what I'm saying."

I know that's her way of taking a shot at me and it is on the tip of my tongue to say, "Well Shad likes it!" but instead of being ignorant I simply smile and say. "Yeah, I do."

After taking their orders I go back to the kitchen and let Pam, my cook know that I have an order for two turkey wraps. "Okay, they will be up shortly." She assures me.

146

Zy is placing fresh baked chocolate chip cookies in the showcase. I am leaning on the counter thinking about what Meechie just said. "What's up? Why are you so quiet?" Zy asks. "Thinking about your boo Shad?"

I automatically start to smile. "Nah, just thinking...nothing in particular." I lie.

"Two turkey wraps with ranch dressing!" Pam yells letting me know that Meechie and Carmen's food is ready.

"Zy can you take that out them for me please?" I ask because I don't have time for Meechie's drama.

"Yeah, I can. Why?"

"I just don't feel like being bothered with them."

She gives me a strange look. "What happened? You were all Ms. Professional when you carried them their drinks. Did one of them say something?"

"Meechie made a slick little comment about getting a turkey wrap so she wouldn't get fat and sloppy. I don't have time for that bullshit Zy, so I am going to stay back here and..."

"And what?" She cut me off. "Look like a coward? Girl, if you don't take those plates out there and smack one of them hookers with it if they say something else to you! You'd better get a backbone! I wish like hell some chick would walk in my place of business and thinks that she is going to disrespect me!"

"I'm not being a coward. I am just avoiding the drama." I correct her.

"No, you are letting this girl feel as if she can come in here and disrespect you and that it's okay! Who is she?"

"Zy, can you just take the plates out please?" I plead with her not wanting to continue this discussion. I am starting to get a headache.

She lets out a frustrated breath and rolls her eyes. "Yeah." She takes Meechie and Carmen out their orders and come back. She looks at me and shakes her head but doesn't say anything. She just continue putting the cookies up. While she is doing that I start wiping down the counter. In the middle of what I am doing Meechie comes up to the counter followed by Carmen, they both have their plates in hand.

"Excuse me but this is nasty!" Meechie blurts holding her plate out to me. I take it.

"Mine doesn't taste good either." Carmen adds from behind her wearing a smirk on her face. I take her plate as well.

"Would you like something else?" I ask politely as I can under the circumstances because they are truly working my nerves.

"Nah." Meechie says with her nose turned up. "That shit that I just ate will probably make me sick and I only took a bite of it!"

"Can you please lower your voice?" I ask still trying to remain calm.

She looks at me like I said something that I wasn't supposed to say. "Excuse you? This is my damn mouth and I will talk as loud as I damn well please! Shit these people sitting up in here knows this food is nasty if they've eaten it! I guess that's why they are reading instead of eating!" She snaps.

"You know what Meechie? It's time for you and your friend to leave! I tried to be nice and act civilized but that's impossible to do when you are dealing with grown children who haven't grown up yet! I knew from the time that you walked in that door that you were only here to pick! I don't have time for the nonsense! I am too old for it and you are as well!"

"First of all bitch, I didn't come here to pick! I came to get something to eat but the shit was nasty! Don't get mad at me because this shit you are serving in here ain't worth feeding to a damn dog!" She is literally screaming! All of my customers are staring and I am so embarrassed.

"Meechie, I am only going to ask you one more time to leave before I call the police!"

"Call'em bitch! Am I supposed to be scared?" She folds her arms defiantly like she is daring me!

"Meechie, let's just leave. You know she's scary as hell anyways, that's why she screaming on calling the cops!" Carmen says and then grabs Meechie by the arm, pulling her towards the door.

"That's alright, I'm going to see your fat ass in the streets bitch and when I do I'm going to bless that ass like I did the last time! Since you want to threaten to call the cops on people! I'm going to give you a reason to call them!" When she gets to the door she stops and yells. "Oh and I hope that you are enjoying my leftovers, you nasty hoe! Shad doesn't want your fat ass! You ain't even his type, he is just using you to try and make me mad!"

"Come on girl." Carmen laughs and pulls Meechie outside.

I am standing behind the register wishing that the floor would open up and I could go through it. I can hear the customers whispering and see them shaking their heads. I take a deep breath and then go over and personally apologize to everyone for the scene that Meechie has just caused. Then I go in the back to my office and close the door because my head is throbbing. A few minutes pass before I hear a knock at the door. "Come in."

Zy peeks her head in. "Are you alright?"

"Yeah, my head is hurting that's all."

"Don't let her get to you. As you can see she is just upset because Shad is with you now. She'll be alright."

"I can't have her coming up here to my place of business like this."

"Nah, you can't. All you have to do is call the police on her the next time that she comes in here but I doubt if she will come back since you have already told her that you will call the police on her. I think that put a little bit of fear in the both of them because when you said police they both dragged ass!" She laughs. I laugh a little bit too thinking back in how Carmen was pulling Meechie towards the door.

"Zy, you are crazy." I joke. "Do me a favor hit that light switch on your way out? I am going to sit here in the dark for a few and relax. Hope this headache will go away."

"Alright boo. Hope you feel better and don't let them girls worry you. They just hate you because they ain't you!" She does her little diva snap and smile. Then she leaves turning off the light and closing the door behind her.

I lay my head on my desk and try to relax but I can't get Meechie's words out of my head. *"Shad doesn't want your fat ass! You ain't even his type, he is just using you to try and make me mad!"*

Shad

Jada and I are sitting in my living room on the sofa. I finally got some furniture. I went down to the Rent-A-Center and got a living room set and a bedroom set. I'd gotten tired of sleeping on that uncomfortable air mattress and having to sit on the floor and watch TV when Jada comes over. I notice that she's been quiet all evening, she came by after she left work.

"What's on your mind Cuteness?" I tease rubbing her thigh. "You have been extra quiet since you got here. That isn't like you, normally your mouth is going a mile a minute." I turn off the TV and face her. "Talk to me."

She lets out a sigh. "I'm good."

I lift her chin and turn her face so that she is looking at me. "Don't lie to me woman. What's on your mind?"

She moves my hand. "Nothing Shad, I'm good."

I can hear in her voice that something is wrong so I ask again. "Jada, what's wrong? And don't say nothing because I can tell that it's something. Come on now spit it out."

She looks up at me. "Meechie and Carmen stopped by my café today. Of course I knew from the time that the walked through the door that they were there to be funny. I didn't say anything though and tried to be civilized. Well that didn't last long because after they got their food they both came up to the register complaining that it was nasty. Meechie was super loud! I asked her to keep her voice down and she went off! She was cursing and acting a fool. Carmen is behind her wearing a smirk the entire time. I didn't argue with her. I simply told her that if she didn't leave I would call the police. She left but before she did she said something that really bothered me."

"And what was that?" I ask. I am already heated at the fact that Meechie had the nerve to go to Jada's job! That is some straight up hoodrat type shit!

"She yells, 'Shad doesn't want your fat sloppy ass! He is just using you to make me mad!' That kind of bothered me. Is that what you are doing? I mean because of course you know that she hates me and nothing would get to her more than you dealing with me." She looks at me waiting for an answer.

I can't believe what just came out of her mouth. "Look let's get one thing straight! I am a grown ass man and I don't have any time to play games with you or anybody else! My time is too valuable to be wasting trying to make Meechie mad or be on some payback type shit! That's what bitches do and I ain't no bitch! I kick it with you because I want to! Because I enjoy being with you! Don't let the dumb shit that comes out of Meechie's mouth poison your mind and have you looking at me sideways! Do I treat you like you are just something to do? Hell, I haven't even tried to have sex with you! I treat you with respect because I feel that's what you deserve. If this was about making Meechie mad then I would've been tried to smash you!"

She is sitting on the sofa looking at me with a dumbfounded expression. "Dag, I'm sorry! I didn't mean it like that!" She stands up. "You don't have to go off on me because I asked a question! If I don't ask then I won't know!"

I stand up too. "I'm not going off on you but I am simply saying that you can't let the crazy shit that somebody else says cloud your judgment! She is obviously miserable as fuck because if she wasn't she wouldn't be worried about what we are doing!"

"I see what you are saying." Jada replies but she has a sad expression on her face. "Maybe I should leave. I'll holla at you tomorrow."

I grab her hand, pulling her close to me. "Don't leave." I use my free hand to move a strand of her hair back out of her face. "I apologize for snapping at you.

Hearing that Meechie came to your job pissed me off and then you believing that stupid shit that she told you mad it worse. That's still no excuse for me yelling at you though. Do you accept my apology?"

Her beautiful grey eyes are locked on mine. "Yeah, I guess."

"What do you mean, you guess?" I ask as I lean down and kiss her soft lips. I can taste her cherry lip gloss. She kisses me back confirming that we're good. "Do you accept my apology or not?" I kiss her again.

Her arms go up around my neck. "I said I guess." She kisses me and I feel my manhood start to rise, pressing against her stomach. She is sucking on my bottom lip. I sit back down on the sofa pulling her down on top of me. She straddles my lap and I am caressing her soft ass. Our tongues dance together and I hear her let out a soft moan. I break our kiss and kiss her on her chin and then move down to her neck. "Shad...you are about to...start something."

"Do you want me to stop?" I ask between kisses.

"Mmmm...god no...but...oh goodness. Wait a minute, I can't think straight with you kissing on my neck like that." She moans, her head is thrown back and her eyes are closed. I kiss my way back up to her lips. We continue kissing until we are both panting and ready to rip each other's clothes off.

"Damn…girl, I want you bad as hell right now." I tell her honestly. "If you aren't ready though we can just chill, I don't want to rush you into anything that you aren't ready for."

"I'm ready but only if you are sure that I am what you really want. Shad, I don't want to get hurt because I am really feeling you. I have been for a while but you already know that." She says looking into my eyes.

"Baby, I would never do anything to hurt you." I promise her.

She gets up from my lap and holds out her hand for me to take. I take her hand and we go down the hall to my bedroom. I undress her kissing every inch of her body as I go. I lay her back on my bed and kiss a trail down her stomach, her legs, and her feet until I reach her toes. I take my time and suck each of her toes.

"Oh damn…Shad…ooooh…lord have mercy!" Jada squeals sitting straight up and looking down at me. I continue to work my magic on her toes; she closes her eyes biting on her bottom lip. Her moans tell me that she is enjoying what I am doing. I leave her feet and kiss my way back up her legs.

"Lay back down." I tell her, I can feel her trembling as I caress her thighs. "Why are you trembling for?"

"I don't know, I guess I'm nervous because this is our first time together." She admits.

I look into her eyes and say. "I got you baby. Just lay back and enjoy." She lies back and I work my tongue magic on her clit while working my two middle fingers in and out of her nice and slowly. In no time she is cumming. Her juices taste like sweet nectar in my mouth. I get her off like this one more time before I reach in the nightstand beside my bed, grab a condom and slip it on. When I slide inside of her it's like I've just slid into heaven. The way that her muscles contract around me sucking me in deeper. I have no choice but to let out a loud moan myself! Damn she feels good!

I lean down sucking and licking her ear. "Damn you feel so good baby." I whisper. "I wish I could stay inside of you forever."

Her nails are in my back and she has her legs wrapped around my waist. "You feel good too. This is even better than I imagined." We kiss passionately as I make love to her. I try my best to prolong my orgasm as long as possible but she feels so good that in no time I am releasing my babies inside of the latex.

Afterwards we lay in each other's arms. I am playing with her hair when she turns to me and say. "Shad, I have never had a man make love to me the way that you just did. I mean the way that you took your time with me." Her eyes roll up in her head. "Mmph...mmph...mmph boy you are something special! I think my legs are still trembling."

I laugh and kiss her on her forehead. "My mission was to please you baby."

"Really? How about we see if you can accomplish it again?" She says seductively challenging me. I don't respond, I just grab another condom and slip it on and then pull her on top of me.

The next morning Jada and I take a shower together and then I cook breakfast for the both of us. We are seated in the living eating, using my coffee table since I still don't have a kitchenette set yet. "How's your food?" I ask referring to the plate of apple pancakes and turkey bacon that is in front of her.

"It's delicious baby. Thank you." She replies. "I think that you are trying to make me fall in love with you Shad Easton."

"I believe that I've already accomplished that Ms. Jada Noels." I wink at her. "Come to think of it, I believe I accomplished that years ago without even trying."

She laughs covering her mouth because she's just put a forkful of pancakes in her mouth. "Oh for real...is that what you believe?"

"Yep." I say confidently knowing that she's had it bad for me for a very long time.

"Whatever big head!"

"I'll be that but you and I both know that I am right."

She playfully rolls her eyes. "I have no idea what you are talking about!"

"Sure you don't." I play along. "So what are your plans for today after you get off from work?"

"I was planning to go and see my parents. I haven't been to visit them in over two weeks and my ma is ready to kick my butt! She doesn't play when it comes to me visiting!"

"Oh okay well that's what's up." I was going to ask her if she wanted to catch a movie or something but that can wait because I'd never try to block her from going to see her people.

"Why did you have something else that you wanted to do?" she is twirling a piece of her curly hair around her finger.

"Not really, was just going to ask if you wanted to go to the movies tonight but you go ahead and see your people. We can go to the movies tomorrow night."

She gets excited like something brilliant just crossed her mind! "I know! Why don't you go with me to visit my parents and then we can go to the movies!"

Meet her parents? I'm not sure if I am ready for that? What if they are stuck up and feel like I am not good enough for her or something? I look at my baby and see how excited she is. I don't want to disappoint her by saying no so I push my silly assumptions aside. "Yeah, that'll work. What time are you planning on going over there?"

"Probably around six."

"Okay, I'll be ready. Do you want to meet here or at your house?"

"My house."

"Okay." I look at my watch and see that it's about time for me to be heading out the door. I get up and take our dishes in the kitchen. When I come back in the living room Jada has her pocketbook and keys. I grab my keys and lunch bag and we walk outside. I put my things in my car and then walk over to her car. I wrap my arms around her and kiss her on her soft lips, looking into her beautiful grey eyes I say. "I am one lucky man. I woke up lying next to the most beautiful woman in Jordan City."

"Well I woke lying next to one of the finest men in Jordan City so I guess that makes me lucky as well." She blushes.

I move a piece of her hair back out of her face. "Stop lying woman, you know I ain't fine! I'm just an ol' ugly ass nigga. Hell I'm lucky that you even looked my way!" I tease.

"Whatever." She smacks her lips. "You're my ol' ugly ass nigga!" We both laugh and share another kiss before I open her car door for her. She gets inside and we say bye to each other. I close her door and remind her to drive safe before getting into my own car and heading to work. On my way to work I give Meechie a call.

Rodney

I am awakened by Meechie arguing on the phone the morning! I haven't been too long gone to sleep because I came in a little after three and then she wanted to stay up and talk my head off. The only way I could shut her mouth was to put my dick in it! Now I still can't get no damn sleep!

"Fuck you and that bitch! I don't give a damn what she came back and told you! She's just mad because I wanted my money back because that food that she served me was nasty and I told her ass so!" She shuts up for a second and I can hear the other person asking her why she is being such an ass! "Fuck you! You're being an ass! You are the one calling me all early in the morning talking about what your bitch came back and told you! What she thought that if she came back and told you it was going to stop me from whooping her ass the next time that I see her? Well it isn't! You ain't my damn daddy! Her scary ass gone threaten to call the cops on me! She better hope she keep them motherfuckas on speed dial because that ass is mines when I see her again and that's my word!" She is bouncing up and down on the bed with her hand all up in the air! No fucking respect for me over here trying to sleep at all! The person on the other end, who

I've figured by now is Shad asks her why is she fucking with some girl named Jada if she has moved on. "I have moved on! I don't care about you or that bitch! I got a man who takes damn good care of me and I am happy so please don't get it twisted boo!"

I have heard enough and is pissed that she woke me up! "Will you please shut the fuck up? I am trying to sleep and I can't with you over there screaming in the phone. Hang that shit up!" I roar ready to slap the shit out of her ass! Not only is she disrespecting me by keeping all of this noise but from what I gather from the argument that she is having with Shad, she's behind my back jocking this nigga's girl. I have the same question as he does. If she's moved on then why in the fuck is she even on this chic like that?

Her neck snaps around and she takes the phone from her ear. "Excuse me?"

"You heard me! Hang up the motherfuckin' phone!" I sit up daring her with my eyes to keep on talking!

"Nigga who..." I slap her so hard she slides off the bed and the phone flies out of her hand landing on the floor!

"I've told you before that I ain't Shad but I see that you want to keep testing me!" I am standing over her, naked as the day that I came into the world. "Why the fuck are you beefing with Shad's bitch?"

This bitch has the audacity to try and kick me in my nuts but I jump back just in time and she misses. She jumps up off the floor and comes at me screaming and swinging like a mad woman! "You sorry motherfucka! You put your hands on me?" She is crying but that shit doesn't faze me at all! I don't feel any remorse for slapping her disrespectful ass!

I grab her and toss her on the bed! "Yeah I put my hands on you! You sitting up in here disrespecting me! If you want to act like a trick then that's how I am going to treat your ass! If you act like a lady then that is how I am going to treat you! I'm over here taking care of your ass and you are worried about Shad and who he's fucking!" She jumps up from the bed and grabs a glass statue that is sitting on the nightstand. She swings it and hits me in the shoulder! She tries to hit me again but I grab her arm and twist it! "Meechie, drop the fucking statue!" I demand! She is tough because she still doesn't drop it! I twist her arm a little harder! "Either you can drop it or I am going to break this motherfucka...your choice!"

She drops the statue and I let go of her arm. "I hate you, you fat fucka! Get the fuck out of my apartment!"

"Girl, you must've forgotten who pays the rent every month!" I remind her.

"I got money motherfucker! I can pay my own rent!"

I laugh. "You got the money that I gave you! Which ain't no more than a few thousand dollars. How long is that going to last?" I give her a few seconds to think about what I have just said. "I can leave though but before I go, I'm going to need the keys to *my* car." I put emphasizes on the word my letting her know that is my shit sitting parked outside!

She is sitting on the bed rubbing her arm, a shocked expression covers her face when I ask for the keys to the car. "Your car?"

"I didn't stutter." I say nonchalantly. I walk around to the other side of the bed and start putting on my clothes.

"Oh so that's how you roll? When you get mad you take back what you gave me? Nigga how are you mad? You put your hands on me!" She jumps up coming around the bed getting up in my face. She looks so pitiful that I do start to feel a little bit bad for hitting her but I can't let her know that. She needs to be broken! She is used to having everything her way and I ain't the nigga to allow that shit! That's why she ran over Shad the way that she did and then when he couldn't continue to give her everything that she wanted anymore she dropped him and ran to me! He was way too soft on her ass! Don't get it twisted, I know that I have some fucked up ways at times but I do care about Meechie. I've had a thing for her for a long time. She's one of the baddest women that I've ever laid eyes on but as I said before I refuse to allow her to do me the way that she did Shad. He made her feel like he couldn't live without her and that the world revolved around Meechie! Well my plan is simple, to make her feel like she can't live without me and so far it's working. I mean, she knows that she can live without me but she can't live the lifestyle that she wants to without me! I don't mind spoiling her or anything because she is my girl and I feel like my woman should have the best of everything if I can afford to give it to her. I don't really care for the money hungry attitude that she has. It's like she wants so much but doesn't feel the need to give anything, not even respect, which is why her ass is delivering packages to Marigold, VA! Normally, I wouldn't ask my woman to do anything like that but the side of her that I started to see when we were in Florida told me that she really isn't here for me at all. It's all about the paper! Like I told her, when she acts like a lady then that's how I will treat her! Until then I am going to treat her like a trick! "Move out of my way, Meechie." I say and brush past her. I walk out of the bedroom and down the hall into the living room. The keys to the car that I bought her are lying on the coffee table I pick them up and put them in my pocket and walk towards the door.

"Give me my keys Rodney!" She demands jumping in front of me.

I stop walking. "I don't have time for this so move. Go ask Shad for the Camry back since you are so worried about what he is doing with ol' girl!" I give her a disgusted look.

"I never said that I was worried about Shad and that bitch!"

"Well if you aren't worried about him and her then why are you beefing with her?" I ask and wait to see what bullshit she will try to spit at me.

"Me and her haven't liked each other for years over some foul shit that she did at a party a few years ago! Yesterday, me and Carmen were downtown and we stopped by her café to get something to eat. The shit was nasty and she got mad because I told her that I didn't want it! Then she tried to pop shit and I told her that I would whoop her ass again so she threatened to call the cops on me if I didn't leave. Obviously she went back and told Shad some bullshit that I was picking at her. So he calls me asking why I went to Jada's job picking!" She explains. "The bitch lied because I wasn't picking!"

I look at her as she is standing in my face lying through her teeth. She must think that I am stupid or something. She could've gone to a million other places to eat but she chose the place where she knows this girl works. "Meechie, get out of my face with that bullshit! You know why you went down there to that girl's spot! Stop trying to play me! It's all good though. Take your ass back to Shad, that way you won't have to be worried about what he's doing with the next bitch!"

She is looking desperate. I know that she ain't really stressing about me leaving. She is stressing about me taking my damn car back! "I'm not worried about Shad and Jada! I could care less about either of them! He was the one who called me with that bullshit!"

I am tired of arguing with her because I see that we aren't getting anywhere. "Listen right now, I'm really not feeling you! You've got a lot of shit with you and I haven't just started to realize it either but this bullshit that I woke up to this morning wasn't cool at all. I am going to leave and give you some time to get your priorities straight."

"What does that supposed to mean?"

"It means I need for you to move from out front of the door." I tell her.

"So you are just going to walk out...just like that? What about us?"

"Move Meechie or I am going to move you myself." I warn.

She reaches out and tries to touch my arm but I snatch away. "Rodney, don't do this? What am I supposed to do?"

"I don't know but right now you need to be moving the hell out of my way so that I can go home and get some sleep since I couldn't get any here!"

"Why is it that every time you get mad, you want to walk out? Why can't we ever talk shit out like two adults? You do this shit every time! I think you do it just so that I can beg you to come back!"

"No, I do it to keep from fucking you up!" I correct. "Now move so I can leave!" She reluctantly moves out of the way and I walk past her out the door. *She'll be alright!* I think to myself as I exit her building and get into my car, leaving her car parked in its spot. I knew that I couldn't drive two vehicles when I took the keys but the point wasn't really to take the car. It was to leave it so her dumb ass can look at it every day parked in the same spot and not be able to drive it! Oh she's going to learn that I run shit!

Meechie

One week later...

The past week has dragged by, I have been trying to get in contact with Rodney but he isn't answering any of my calls. I'm confused as to why he feels as though he has a reason to be so upset with me. I understand him being upset after overhearing what had gone down between Jade and I but I feel like I am the one who should be upset and ignoring him. That nigga put his hands on me! I guess he feels what I did was wrong but him putting his hands on me is cool! I've been doing a lot of thinking this week and I am starting to feel like fucking with Rodney was a big mistake! Him hitting me told me that he doesn't care about me like I thought that he did because if a man loves a woman then he would never hit her. I've come to the conclusion that I am just going to focus on getting as much money out of his ass as I can and save it so that once my account is straight I can drop his ass and be straight for a while until I meet another sucka! Hopefully I can find one before I drop his ass! That way I won't have to be worried about how my bills are going to be paid or having to work at some minimum wage paying job! I am about to be on some straight fuck niggas type of shit! It's all about Meechie from here on out! As a matter of fact fuck everybody if your name ain't Meechie!

I also realized that Douglas was right about the things that he said about Rodney because since then I've made two more trips out to Marigold. He even had the nerve to ask me for half of the money! At first he'd said that I could keep all of the money but now I only keep half! Douglas had a smirk on his face the second time that I went like he wanted to say, 'I told you so.' But he didn't as a matter of fact he was really nice to me, he even gave me a thousand dollar tip. He did the same thing on the last trip that I made a few weeks ago. So far I have a little over seven thousand saved up but that ain't no real money for someone who likes to spend like I do. I have a plan though...

I pick up my cell and stroll through my contacts until I come to Carmen's number. I press send and wait for her to answer. While I am waiting for her to pick up I walk over to the window and peek out of the blinds. I look at my car sitting parked in the same spot that it has been sitting in all week and want to kick myself for not getting a duplicate made! I'd already given Rodney the spare so when he took the main key that left me with nothing. *How could I have been so stupid?* I think to myself.

"Hello." Carmen answers, interrupting my thoughts.

"Hey girl" I close the blinds and walk across the room and flop down on the sofa. "I hate to keep bothering you because I know that you have shit of your own to do but I need a favor." I inform her, honestly not caring about what she has to do. Like I said from here on out everything is about me. Call it selfish but I really don't give a damn! I've learned that most motherfuckers are all about themselves in this world, so why should I be any different?

"Nah, you're good girl." She replies. "I wasn't doing anything but folding some clothes. And you know goodness well that I don't mind doing anything that I can to help you in any way that I can. What's up?"

Pleased with her response I say. "I need you to take me by Shad's job. I hate to have to ask his ass for anything but I need for him to lend me the car. I should've never given it back to his ass!" *Another stupid move that I made!*

She was quiet for a moment like she was contemplating whether or not she should take me. "I'll take you but don't go down there fussing with him because you saw how things turned out when we went by Jada's café! I ain't got time for him or his supervisor to be threatening to call the cops on our asses over that raggedy ass car!"

173

"Child boo...ain't nobody thinking about Shad or his whack ass supervisor! I'm not going to be arguing with him. If he says that I can't use the car then I'm just going to leave! Plain and simple because I'm certainly not about to beg him. Nah ain't none of that popping off!" I assure her meaning every word that I am saying.

"Alright then, let me put these clothes away and I'll be over there in a few." She says. I tell her that will be fine and we hang up.

I go in the bathroom, take a shower and then get dressed. I choose a khaki Roca Wear jumper dress that stops just below my ass cheeks and a pair of black sandals. I untie my hair and comb down my wrap and then apply a little bit of lip gloss to my lips. I notice that there is still a light bruise on the side of my face from where Rodney hit me. Its cleared up a lot but you can still see it some. I hope that Shad doesn't notice it because I don't feel like explaining what happened. I also don't want him looking at me like 'that's what your ass get for choosing that nigga over me'. I give myself the once over in the mirror to make sure that I am looking good and is please with my reflection.

Forty-five minutes later, Carmen and I are pulling into the parking lot at Shad's job. I see the Camry parked next to a fly ass power blue Dodge Charger sitting on some twenty-two's. I wonder to myself which one of these niggas

working here is driving it and also what are they doing that Shad isn't to be able

to afford a ride like that. "I'll be right back." I tell Carmen getting out of the car

and switching my ass inside like I belong here. I walk inside to the main office and

is greeted by David.

"Hello, pretty lady. How are you today?" He asks openly checking me out.

"I'm doing just fine. How about yourself?" I reply politely but really couldn't

give a damn! He's sitting here trying to be cool and flirt with me looking like he's

been beat in the face with a bag of nickels. He has the worst case of acne that I've

ever seen and craters all over his face! To top it all off his teeth are jacked up and

crooked as hell!

"I'm living so I can't complain." He replies licking his lips and leaning back in

his chair. "Let me guess, you're here to see Shad?"

"Yes, can I please?" I give him a phony smile.

"Yes, you can doll baby. You can have anything that you want." He gets up

from his chair. "I'll go and get him for you but before I do. I must say he was a fool

for letting you get away. If you ever need anything and I do mean *anything* you just give me a call." He hands me his business card with all of his numbers listed on it including his home phone, I take it and slip it in one of the pockets on my jumper. When he turns to walk away I roll my eyes up in my head. *This old fool must be smoking if he believes that he will be hearing from me!*

David returns a few minutes later with Shad strolling along beside him. The expression on Shad's face tells me that he isn't happy to see me.

"What's up?" He asks dryly. I can tell that he's just gotten a fresh haircut and shape up recently. Even though I'm not feeling him right now I must admit that this is one fine motherfucka! I think about him being with Jada and my pressure instantly rises but I know that I can't let that show. I am here for a favor so showing my ass is not an option.

"Hey, can I speak to you privately please?" I ask glancing at David.

"Yeah we can step outside but I don't have long. I have work to do." He says matter-of-factly, not bothering to try and hide his ill feelings towards me.

"Okay." I lead the way outside being sure to put a little extra swing in my hips in case he's watching. When we get outside I decide to apologize to him before asking for the car hoping that will increase my chances of getting it. "Shad,

I know that you and I are not on good terms right now and I hate that. I really wish that..."

"Meechie, what do you want?" He rudely interrupts me. "I told you that I don't have all day."

I want more than anything to cuss his ass out right now but I bite my tongue and stay in character! I continue, "I just want to say that I am sorry for everything that has happened."

"Cool." He turns and grabs the handle on the door to go back inside. I grab his arm.

"Hold on. I need to use the car for a couple of days to look for another job." I lie.

He looks at me in disbelief and began to chuckle. "I knew your ass wanted something! Talking about...*I just wanted to apologize for everything that has happened!* Girl, get the hell out of here with that bullshit! Besides, you gave my car back when you upgraded so why can't you drive the car that Rodney bought you?"

"It's broke down." I lie again. "I don't know what's wrong with it, it won't start."

He shakes his head. "Sounds like a personal problem to me!" he retorts.

Time for some water works! "Shad please, I know that you are upset with me but I really need you to lend me the car." I plead with fake tears in my eyes. He has never been able to see me cry without giving in.

For the first time he turns and looks at me, he opens his mouth to say something but then his expression changes. He grabs my face and turns it to the side where the bruise is. "What the fuck happened to your face?" He explodes.

Caught off guard, I began to stutter. "Umm-umm..umm..."

"Umm-umm my motherfuckin' ass! What happened to your face?" He is screaming and the big vein in the middle of his forehead is bulging out. "Did that nigga put his hands on you, Meechie?"

"N-no...no Shad it wasn't like that." I realize that I have been lying since I stepped out of the car. I have to admit that I'm loving the fact that he is mad at the thought that Rodney may have hit me. That tells me that even though we are on bad terms and he's with Jada, he still loves me.

178

"What you mean it wasn't like that?" He asks still holding my face in his grip. "Did that nigga hit you, yes or no?"

From behind me I hear Carmen yell! "What the hell are you doing holding her face like that Shad? Let her go!" She demands.

Shad turns me a loose and just as quickly he is all in Carmen's shit! "Yo mind your damn business!" He is walking towards her pointing his finger in her face and she is backing up wearing a terrified expression.

"Shad calm down!" I plead with him tugging on his arm in hopes of keeping him from slapping the piss out of Carmen. "She was just making sure that I was good." I look past him to Carmen. "Girl, I'm good. You can go back and wait for me in the car." She doesn't bother to respond. She turns on her heels and makes her way back to the car.

"If she is so worried about you being good then where in the fuck was she when that nigga was smacking you upside the head?" Shad yells after Carmen, making sure that she hears every word that he is saying.

"Is everything alright out here?" That's David peeking his head outside the door, looking from me to Shad in an attempt to figure out what is going on.

"Yes everything is fine, David." I give him a nervous smile.

"Yeah, everything is good." Shad confirms. "I'll be in, in a few minutes. I won't be much longer."

"Alright. Try to keep it down out here." He tells Shad before going back inside.

Shad has calmed down some. "What happened to your face?"

"We were playing around and he accidently hit me too hard. I told you that it wasn't like you were thinking."

He looks at me unconvinced as though he can see right through the lie I just fed him. "That's bullshit and you know it but I'll accept that...at least until I see Rodney. For his sake he'd better pray that y'all have the same story."

Instead of replying, I ask. "Can I get the car?" He reaches in the front pocket of his overalls and hands me the key. "Do you need me to come back and pick you up when you get off?"

"Nah, I'm good." He says and then grabs the door to go back inside. He stops and looks back at me. "Is it worth it?"

"Huh?" I ask confused.

"The paper…is it worth you walking around with bruises on your face?"

I drop my head unable to look him in the eyes at this point because I can see the disappointment that is written all over his face. "I told you that we were playing."

"Yeah, I know." With that he walks back inside.

I walk back over to Carmen's car, where she is sitting inside with the windows rolled up and the doors locked. When she rolls the window down, I burst into laughter. "For real Carmen, why in the hell are you sitting in the car with the doors locked?"

"Bitch fuck you!" She snaps. "Did you see how mad he was? He was ready to kill my ass!"

I roll my eyes up in my head as I continue to laugh. "Girl stop! That boy was not about to do nothing to your overly dramatic ass! He was just upset that's all. Everything is all good. He gave me the car!" I hold up the key giving it a little shake.

"Good now get your ass in it and let's go or you can stay! It doesn't matter to me but I am taking my black ass back to Cedar Place Avenue! Every time that I go somewhere with you something bad happens!"

"Girl, stop whining!" She is really beginning to get on my nerves! I love Carmen to death and she is really like a sister to me being that we grew up together, living next door to each other in the same apartment complex. Sometimes she just plucks my nerves she can take small shit and make a big deal out of it. She is acting as if Shad put his hands on her or something.

"Whatever! What are you about to do?" She asks pulling down the sun visor and fixing her hair in the mirror.

"I'm about to go by Rodney's house and see if I can catch up with his ass being that he isn't answering his damn phone!"

"Girl, you are better than me because if he didn't want to talk to me then I wouldn't stress it. I would be looking for a job! You don't need him, Meechie." She puts the visor back up and looks at me. I'd told her about what happened between Rodney and me. "There isn't enough money in the world for me to let a man beat my ass!"

I smack my lips. "He didn't beat my ass! He hit me and I hit his ass back!" I corrected.

"Okay whatever, the point is that he put his hands on you and you are acting as if it's cool. Forget that mess! You need to leave him alone and do you! If he was trifling enough to hit you once then he'll do it again!"

I shake my head disagreeing with her. "Nah, I ain't worried about that!"

She lets out a frustrated breath. "Why don't you ever listen to anybody? I am trying to tell you something for your own good! When did you turn into this chick that is willing to do anything for money except work?"

She is starting to sound like Shad now! I'm getting fed up with people trying to tell me how to live my life! If I don't want to work and have a man take care of me then I feel like that's my business! I've tried that nine to five shit and it just isn't for everybody, especially not me! Hell there is men who do the same shit, lay-up and have a woman take care of them! "Listen, you don't have to agree with my choices and decisions because you don't have to live with them...I do." I say tapping my index finger against my chest. "Everybody is acting as if I am killing somebody or something. Besides are you forgetting that I do work? I do my lil drop off for Rodney when he needs me to out in Marigold..."

"Exactly! You risk your damn freedom every time Rodney needs you to! All because you are too damn lazy to work and take care of your own damn self! If that nigga loved you or cared anything for you, he wouldn't be asking you to do that shit! If you ask me he's making you work for the shit that he gives you! You told me that it was supposed to be a onetime thing but obviously that was some bullshit that he told you in order to get you to do it!" She pauses for a second and then continues. "All I am saying Meechie is...wake up and get your shit together before it's too late because from what I am seeing you are making a mess! Look at how Shad went off after seeing your face. Now who's to say that when he sees Rodney he isn't going to step to him for putting his hands on you? Then those two will be fighting! This shit just gets messier and messier."

"Are you done?" I said with obvious attitude. "You done gave me a damn headache with all of your preaching!"

"Yeah, I'm done but since you don't want to listen to me, don't call me when this shit gets out of hand!" She starts her car and backs out of the parking lot.

I get in my car and head to Rodney's house.

Rodney

Me and Demetrius are riding around getting blowed when my cell phone

starts to ring. I look at the screen and see Meechie's name flashing on the screen.

I hit ignore and then take another toke of the blunt before passing it to him. My

phone goes off again letting me know that I have a text message. I open the

message and read it. It's a message from Meechie telling me that she's at my crib

and that she really needs to talk to me so that we can straighten things out. I lay

my phone back in my lap after reading her message. "I'll tell you man, bitches are

a trip." I say to Demetrius.

"Shiiiit...you ain't telling me nothing that I don't already know. That's why I

fuck'em and keep it moving! I ain't trying to cuff none of these nasty bitches." He

replies offering me the blunt back. I shake my head no and he puts it out in the

ashtray. "These women now a days are only out for what they can get and on top

of that they ain't willing to do shit for you in return! I mean to keep it one

hundred, I don't need no bitch to bust nut! I can do that by myself! They feel like

if they lay down and spread their legs you are automatically obligated to take care

of their asses. Don't get me wrong, I doing nothing for my woman but her ass gotta be doing something to deserve that shit. I need her to be cooking, cleaning, washing my clothes and taking care of me like my mama used to do my pops. My pops never came home to a dirty house and his dinner was always on the table, hot and waiting for him. In return he made sure that the bills were paid and that she had everything that she wanted and needed. These women these days don't know nothing about that! They are too busy trying to look fly and keep up with the next bitch and in everybody's business!"

I nod my head in agreement. He'd taken the words right out of my mouth. "Man who you telling? You know that I've been digging Meechie for a minute. I've always felt like she could do better than Shad's ass so when I saw her and she told me that shit was over between the two of them. I felt like I was finally going to get my chance to show her how a woman is supposed to be treated. You know how I roll, I love to have nice shit and I feel like my woman should too. Everything was cool at first, you know she had her little job down at Walmart and shit. She'd told me that she wasn't really feeling it though. Of course I was like even if she doesn't work I would make sure that she was taken care of but the more that I sit back and observe shit I see more and more that she doesn't want to do anything but spend my money. She doesn't do anything that a woman does for her man. I can't even tell you if this girl can cook because we've been together now for over five

186

months and she's never cooked me shit! We never sit down and talk. The only words that she ever says to me are, 'Baby, I need some money so that I can get this or that'. I feel like she's trying to play me for some kind of sucka and if that's what she's thinking then she'd better think again because she has the game fucked up. She just don't seem to be about nothing, that's why I have her ass making runs out to Marigold for me! Ain't shit free…you feel me? If she wants to spend it, she's going to earn it one way or another. Point blank." I decide to keep it all the way real with my boy as to why I am really starting to feel the way that I am about Meechie. "Check it out, when we went to Florida, I overheard her ass on the phone bragging to one of her hoodrat ass friends about how much money I'd spent on her and how she had no plans of going back to school or working. Her trifling ass even had the nerve to say, 'I give him pussy and head when he wants it so I am doing my job.' Can you believe that shit?"

He laughs. "Yeah, I can believe it! I told you that's the way these bitches be thinking!"

"Then on top of that, last week when I was over at her crib. She woke me up on the phone arguing with Shad because she'd gone down to his girl's job trying to start some shit with her. The girl went back and told him about it so he called to ask Meechie why she had done it. She swore up and down that she hadn't been picking at ol' girl but if she wasn't picking then she wouldn't have went to that girl's job! Man, she made me so fucking mad that I slapped her disrespectful ass before I knew it! I even took the keys back to the car I bought her ass! I told her that if she is so worried about Shad then her ass needs to go back and get that raggedy ass car that he gave her!"

"Sounds to me like you just need to leave her ass alone!" He tells me as we pull up in his driveway.

"Yeah, I don't really have time for her shit!"

"Have you heard anything about Crawl, since what happened?" he asks changing the subject.

Truth be told I have been laying low, trying not to cross paths with Crawl. I haven't been near the eastside since the shit that happened but I ain't no fool and I know that the shit is still a long ways from over. "Nah, I haven't heard anything. That nigga ain't trying to see me for real because if he was he knows where I be." I grab the roach from the ashtray and put some fire to it. I take a toke an inhale the weed smoke into my lungs before releasing it slowly through my nose and mouth.

"I hear that but I don't think you are trying to see him either!" Demetrius teases but I don't find shit funny!

"What are you trying to say?" I ask feeling some type of way about his slick ass comment.

He throws up his hands still laughing. "Calm down killa, I'm just fucking with you! I didn't mean any harm." He stops laughing and his expression becomes serious. "On some real shit though, you know his reputation and you know that when he sees you it's going to be a problem."

I wave him off. "Man, fuck that nigga. The next time that we cross paths I ain't going to be on no talking shit. You feel me?" He just nods his head. "Well anyways, I have a few more moves to make. I'm about to slide on up out of here."

"Alright then holla at me later." He says getting out of the car.

"Alright." I put the car in reverse and back out. On my way across town my phone rings again. I look at the screen and again, it's Meechie. This time I answer. "Yo."

"It's about time you answer your phone." She says in a whiny voice. "I'm parked outside your house. How long will it be before you get here?"

"I don't know."

"What do you mean, you don't know? We need to talk Rodney." She pleads. "I miss you."

"I don't have shit to talk about! You are disrespectful and all you care about is your damn self! You can cut all of the bullshit Meechie, you don't miss me. You miss that car and my money." She is quiet, guess the cat has her fucking tongue now! "Yeah, I overheard your ass on the phone when we were in Miami, bragging about all of the money that I'd spent on you and how you didn't plan on going back to school. I heard all of that shit! You aren't the type of chick that I thought you were, you are a gold-digging, money hungry bitch! You are all about what you can get and that's it!"

"Rodney, that's not true!" She insists! "Yes you did hear me on the phone telling Carmen about all of the things that you had given me but it wasn't like you think! I was just rubbing it in her face how my man had spoiled me. As far as school, yes I'll admit that I never had any plans on going back because I never liked school even when my ass was there! I just didn't know how to tell you that I didn't want to go back because you seemed so adamant about it!"

I know that she is only running game because her ass misses my money but it's cool because I need her to keep making these runs for me! "I'm busy right now but I'll swing by later." I don't even give her a chance to respond before I disconnect the call. I drive over to this little burger joint over on Pine St. I park my car and go inside. I am standing up at the register looking over the menu, when a female voice says.

"Have you nearly run over anyone today?"

I turn to see the chick that I nearly hit a couple months ago. Today she is dressed in a purple and white tight fitting top with a pair of white skin tight jeans on. She's bad as hell too, a thick lil redbone. She looks young as hell though. "Hey lil mama." I laugh at her comment. "Nah, I haven't nearly hit anyone today. Most people crossing the street look both ways before crossing."

She laughs too revealing deep dimples in both of her cheeks. "Oh okay, I guess you're right about that but I had a lot on my mind that day."

"You look too young to have a lot on your mind. How old are you anyways?" I ask. Before she can respond the guy at the register clears his throat. "Yo, my man is there a problem with your throat?"

"You two need to order or get out of line so that the next person can order!"

"You need to check your fucking tone!" I snarl at him pointing my finger in his face. I throw the menu across the counter. "I don't even want shit!" I turn to walk away from the counter, the little redbone is staring at me wearing a shocked expression. "You can roll with me to get something from somewhere else if you want." I offer.

"Cool." She gladly accepts.

When we get outside, I ask. "Where is your whip?"

"I'm not driving."

"Oh okay." I hit the button on the remote that's on my keychain to unlock the doors. We get in and I head downtown. "You know I didn't even get your name. That whack ass nigga back there plucked my nerves before I had a chance to."

"I'm Tia." She replies, seeming a bit nervous since we got in the car.

"I'm Rodney. You're a bad lil chick." I lick my lips glancing over at her. The top she has on is low cut and her firm breasts are spilling out of it. They look so smooth that I briefly imagine what they would feel and taste like. "How old are you?"

"I'm seven...I meant eighteen." She stutters.

"Which one is it? Either you are seventeen or you're eighteen."

"I'm eighteen. I just had a birthday and so that's why I almost said seventeen." She explains.

"Oh okay. That's what's up. That means that you are legal." I smile glad to hear that. She smiles back. I put my hand on her thigh. "Relax baby girl, you seem a little bit nervous. You are in good hands."

"I'm not nervous, I'm good." She assures me.

Jada

I am at the café giving ZyKia a few last minute instructions before I leave. "Don't forget to set out the new magazines that just came in and we also got in a new shipment of books today. Make sure you set them out as well. If you don't feel like it ask Netta to do it."

"Girl, I have everything here under control. You can go ahead home." She assures me pushing me towards the door. "Go and see your man or something!"

"Oh hush, I know that you have everything. I am just reminding you that's all." My cell rings, I look at the screen and see that it's Shad. A smile immediately spreads across my lips. I press send to answer and put the phone up to my ear. "Hey baby." I coo into the phone.

"Hey baby." He sounds tired. "Can you pick me up from work when you get off? I hate to bother you but I'm tired as shit and I don't feel like walking."

I'm confused as to why he would be walking instead of driving his car. "What's wrong with your car?"

I hear him let out an exasperated breath. "I'll tell you when you get here."

Not really liking the sound of his response, I say. "Is everything okay?"

"Yeah, everything's good." He says unconvincingly.

I can hear in his voice that something is wrong but I don't continue to press. He said that he would tell me when I get there so I'll wait to find out then. "Alright well, I'll be there in about twenty minutes."

"Alright." I hang up the phone and tell ZyKia that I am about to leave.

"Alright, drive safely and call me later if you're not busy."

"Okay." I throw my pocketbook on my shoulder and head uptown to pick up Shad. On the way over there I can't help but wonder what has happened to his car. I know for sure that it's paid for so it hasn't been repossessed. He couldn't have been in an accident because he wouldn't have called and asked me to pick him up from work. Different scenarios cross my mind but none of them makes sense.

When I pull up in the parking lot at Shad's job, he is standing outside talking to one of his co-workers. They continue to talk for another minute or so before they end their conversation and he walks over and get in the car with me. I can immediately tell by the expression on his face that my suspicions about something being wrong are correct. "Hey baby." He leans over and kisses me. Then he reclines the seat back and close his eyes.

"Long day?" I ask ready to find out what the heck is going on.

"Nah, not really."

"Oh...well where's your car?"

"Meechie has it." He replies.

Not prepared for that response, I ask. "Why does Meechie have your car? I thought that you told me she has a new one."

He sits his seat up and looks over at me. "She does, she said that it broke down and she needed to borrow the Camry to go and handle some business."

"Why is that your problem? Doesn't she have a boyfriend with a car and so she claims an ass load of money?" I don't try to hide my attitude at all! I am so sick of Meechie! It seems like as soon as I think that she is out of the picture and has finally moved on, he lets her right back in! I am not trying to be mean and I am not insecure at all! It's just that Meechie is a drama queen and she loves to keep something started. I refuse to have a relationship filled with drama! I love Shad but I won't deal with Meechie!

"Why are you asking me all of these damn questions? I let her use the car, what's the big deal?" He snaps. "I mean damn you acting like I said that I fucked the girl or something!"

He has never snapped at me like this before so I am taken aback by his attitude towards me. "You're right, there is no big deal. It's your car, you can let whoever you want borrow it!" I want to add, *you should've called Meechie to take your ass home!* Instead I keep my mouth closed and look straight ahead at the traffic. My frustration is on one thousand right about now!

When we get to Shad's place, I pull up in front of his apartment but don't turn off the ignition. "Aren't you going to come in?"

"Nah, I'm going home."

"So what you mad at me for letting Meechie use the car?" He asks like that is a damn trick question or something.

"Nope."

He lets out a long sigh. "Jada, why are you trippin'?"

"I'm not, I'm good." I assure him. "You are the one who got bent all out of shape because I said that her car breaking down is no longer your problem. She has a boyfriend let him worry about her car breaking down!"

"Look I don't feel like arguing about this. She has the car now so really us arguing about it is pointless. I honestly don't understand why you are making such a big deal about it."

I turn some in my seat to look at him. "The big deal is you need to let Meechie and her problems go! She is your past, from what you tell me that is what she chose! So I feel like that if she doesn't have a ride or whatever the problem maybe then she needs to figure shit out on her own not run to you because that is going to cause problems with us. She's not going to be popping up whenever she feels like it!"

"Are you telling me who the hell I can and cannot deal with?"

"Nah baby, I am telling you what I will and will not deal with!" I look him directly in his eyes as I speak. "If you want to play captain save-a-hoe then go right ahead but I'm not going to stick around for it. Meechie is miserable and everybody knows that misery loves company. I refuse to allow her to make me miserable...y'all can have that."

"You are really over-reacting over something that isn't that serious! If the shoe was on the other foot and you needed my help, I would've done the same damn thing!"

"You can sit there and play dumb all you want to like you don't know what I am saying but I mean what I said. If you are going to continue to deal with her then you won't be dealing with me!"

"Whatever, I don't have time for this shit!" He says before getting out of the car and slamming the door.

I put my car in reverse and leave. I don't feel bad at all for saying how I feel. I know how Meechie is and so does he. He just allows his love for her to cloud his judgment! I can see right through her ass! I bet if he needed her she wouldn't help him. Where was she when he was walking home from work before I came into the picture? Where was she when he needed someone to help him move? Where has she been when he needed anything? Somewhere thinking about her damn self! Everything is about her! The only time that she comes around is when she wants something or wants to start something! Jada Noels isn't about to deal with the bullshit! I love Shad but until he can completely move on from Meechie. He doesn't have to worry about me!

Jada

The next night after work, ZyKia and I decided to go out to a local bar for drinks. We are seated at a table near the back enjoying Blue Motorcycles, chips and dip. "Girl, I needed this?" I say moving my hair from my face. "This thing with me and Shad is really bothering me. I hate that we aren't talking but Zy, I can't keep dealing with Meechie in and out of his life! She ain't nothing but a little selfish, immature, drama queen! It's not about me trying to tell him who he can or cannot deal with. It's about me refusing to deal with a whole lot of drama. You saw how she acted that day when she and her friend Carmen came in...totally uncalled for!"

Zy nods her head in agreement as she takes a sip of her drink. "Yeah she is a ghetto hot mess but he is going to have to get fed up with her mess and decided to stop dealing with her on his own. You telling him will only cause him to get defensive like he did because he feels that you are trying to tell him what to do."

"I'm sorry if he feels like I am trying to tell him what to do because that is really not the case. I just can't have a relationship with him if he is going to continue to deal with her. Hell, he has problems of his own that he needs to be worried about instead of trying to help her." I finish off my drink and wave the waitress over. Me and Zy both order another Blue Motorcycle. We sit and continue to discuss my relationship a while longer and end up having another round of drinks. By the end of my third Blue Motorcycle, I am starting to feel the effects of the alcohol and I can tell that Zy is as well.

"Girl, stop worrying about Shad and let's go somewhere where we can dance! Everything will work itself out!" Zy suggests. I really don't feel like going home yet so I agree. We pay our tab and then drive across town to a club called Changez.

"How do I look?" I ask Zy as we step out of the car. I'm now wondering if I should've chosen the short tight gold halter dress that I am wearing.

"Girl, you look great as usual! Shoot with all of them hips and booty that's popping out of that dress, we might get in free!" She teases.

I tug at the bottom of my dress trying to pull it down some. I don't want to be out here looking like no hoe! "Is it too short?"

Zy grabs me by the arm pulling me in the direction of the club! "Bring your ass on here! By the time you get through asking questions they will be closing! You look fine!"

We pay our ten dollar admission fee at the door and make our way inside of the crowded club. It's packed! "Alright now, I came to dance and have a good time so there will be no sitting or standing against the wall!" Zy announces yelling over the music. "Let's get out there on the dance floor and show these fine ass brothers what we are working with!" We head to the dance floor. The music is jumping and the two of us are having a ball. We stay on the floor until the lights come on! It has been a while since I've been out but I have definitely enjoyed myself. Zy and I are both sweaty, our hair stuck to our faces and sweat dripping down our bodies.

As everyone is filing out of the club, the guy that Zy has been dancing with all night asks her if he can get her number. We are standing outside of the club and I am waiting while the two of them are talking and exchanging numbers. I hear someone say. "Ain't that the bitch that Shad fucks with right there?"

I look next to me and see Meechie, Nikki and some other girls standing in a little group. There are a few people standing between us separating us. "Yeah, that's that bitch!" Meechie slurs looking directly at me. "I ain't gone say shit to her though because she ain't gone do nothing but run back and tell Shad like she did the last time! Ol' scary ass bitch!"

Her little crew all erupts in laughter. "I know that's right girl." Nikki instigates. "Don't you just hate them scary type bitches that are scared to handle dey business like a woman? Instead dey go running to the next mothafucka telling shit!"

"Giiiiirrrlll, tell me about it." One of the other girls says.

I am finding it hard to keep my composure as I listen to this pack of rats talk shit about me in my face. This is exactly the type of shit that I was trying to explain to Shad about Meechie, bottom line she is a rat who loves drama! "Zy, let's go." I call to my friend who is in a deep conversation with the brother who asked for her number.

"Okay, in a minute." She replies never taking her eyes off of ol' boy.

"I'm ready to go now, Zy!" I snap letting her know that it's time to go.

"Yeah bitch, do what you always do...run!" Meechie yells as I am walking off. "I'm willing to bet the hair on my head that Shad will be calling me first thing in the morning asking me what I've said to you now!"

"You know her ass is going to run back and tell it!" Nikki chimes in. "She's just trying to get him mad with you to secure her little spot in his life!"

I stop walking and turn around. "Meechie, why don't you grow the fuck up?" I ask walking back in their direction. The alcohol that I have consumed has me feeling fearless! At this moment right here I am ready for anything! If she wants to pop off we can do that! Fuck turning the other cheek! I am tired off putting up with her shit! Zy is now beside me asking what is going on but I ignore her! "Every time that you see me somewhere you are always on some petty shit, you and these petty ass rats that you run with! If you don't like me, I personally don't give a damn! You don't have to but you are not going to keep picking at me everywhere you see me!"

Meechie gets all animated, looking around, waving her arms and swinging her head from side to side! "Oh hell nah, I know this bitch ain't talking to me! Somebody must've given this hoe a sip of gorilla juice or something that's got her feeling tough! I will say whatever the fuck I want, whenever I want! What are you going to do about it?"

We are face to face now! My heart is beating fast and my adrenaline is pumping. "We can do whatever! I'm not scared of you, Meechie!" I let her know! She pushes me and I push her ass right back! Before either of us can swing several bouncers get between us.

"Both of you need to get off of the premises right now before we have to call the police!" One of the bouncers announces.

"Come on Meechie, that bitch ain't worth you going to jail for!" Nikki yells.

"Shut the fuck up and mind your business Nikki! You always got your mouth in something!" I yell trying to break a loose from the bouncer that is holding me! "I am sick of y'all bitches! I don't bother anybody but y'all are constantly fucking with me!" I've never been so mad in my entire life! Tears are streaming down my face! I know that if I break loose from this bouncer they will more than likely jump me but honestly I don't care. This is one ass whopping I will proudly take! This shit has to end!

"Calm down Jada and let's go!" Zy is pleading with me!

205

"Bitch you don't really want him to let go of you!" Meechie barks! "You are acting like you really want to do something! You know just like I do what happened the last time! You don't want a repeat of that ass whooping!"

Her words just infuriate me more and I try harder to break away from the bouncer that is holding me! "Let's do it then Meechie!"

Nikki and her crew are laughing and still egging it on. "Let's go Meechie, that hoe is just mad because at the end of the day you will always have Shad's heart, she knows she is just a fucking fill-in!"

"And is!" Meechie laughs. "You ought to be thanking me bitch for allowing you to have him because if I wanted to I could take him from your bouji ass! You know just like I do where his heart is! He doesn't want you! You ain't even his type! He doesn't like bouji bitches! He's only fucking with you because he knows that I can't stand your ass! It's sad to see how he playing with your feelings knowing damn well if I call he's gonna come running!"

"Ignore her and let's go!" Zy says to me.

"Ma'am, you had better listen to your friend because if you don't stop arguing with her and struggling against me. I am going to have you arrested! Now get in your car and leave!" The bouncer says sternly.

"Fine just let me go! I'm leaving!" I snap!

I hear the other bouncers warning Meechie and her crew as Zy and I are walking in the direction of my car. "Do you see what I was saying now?" I am venting to her. "This is the shit right here that I was talking about! Fuck Shad and this bullshit! I can't do this shit! He can have that bitch because they are both simple as hell!"

"I'll drive." Zy offers as we approach my car. "You are too upset to be driving." I give her the keys and get in on the passenger side. As we drive in the direction of Zy's house, the car is quiet except for my sniffles. "Don't cry Jada, I know that you are sick of this mess and you don't deserve it! That girl only messes with you like that because she is jealous of you! She sees how beautiful, smart, successful and driven you are and she is jealous. So is the rest of the little rat pack that she runs with! It's sad that grown ass women behave like that but they will be alright. Don't let the mess that she said about Shad get to you either. She knows that you aren't just a fill-in. The only reason that she said that dumb mess was because she thought that it sounded cute! She was trying to impress her friends!"

"That may be true but the part about him going every time that she calls is true! That I can't deal with! I'm just over anything involving that girl and he should be too! I mean what is it about that bitch that he can't let go of?" I am puzzled because I can't understand why any man would want to waste his time on her!

"Well Jada, it's simple in spite of all that she has done. He still loves her. I am not saying that he want to be with her because I don't think that at all. I have seen the two of you together and I can tell that he is really digging you. It's just one of those situations where he is so used to being there for her that it's hard for him to turn his back on her when she comes to him for help." She explains. "Shad is a good guy that just got involved with the wrong type of chic, one who doesn't appreciate the kind of man that he is and that uses any and everybody that she comes in contact with in order to get what she wants. Don't worry though he is going to reach his breaking point with her and tell her ass to kick rocks! You'll see."

"I doubt if I'll see it because I doubt if I'll be around." I look out the window at the streets. "All I want is to be happy Zy...that's all. I don't want or need this drama."

"I feel you." We drive in silence the rest of the way to her house.

Meechie

I wake up the next morning with a headache after getting home from the club a little after four. I roll over and look at the clock on my nightstand it reads 11:46am. I throw back the covers and go into the bathroom to empty my bladder while I am sitting on the toilet I reach over and turn on the water in the shower. When I am done using the bathroom, I flush the toilet, get undressed and step inside the shower. As the warm water runs over my head and cascades down my body, I think back to the argument that Jada and I had outside of the club this morning! I get a little tickled when I think back to how she was trying to go all hard like she really wanted to do something! Yeah picture that! Jada know she ain't ready for me! I guess she was just trying to show off because there were so many people watching! I swear I hate that bitch with everything in me! I've tried to get past how I feel about her but I can't! Every time that I see her I want to beat her ass! It's worse than it was before because now she's fucking with Shad! I know I shouldn't care because we are not together and he has the right to be with anyone that he chooses but not her! I kind of feel like this bitch is laughing on the inside because even though I whooped her ass in the past she still ended up getting him! It's like she still got the last laugh! I don't like that shit at all. I will

never forget the way that she turned her nose up at me that night at the party

and told Shad that he could do better than me! I hate bitches who think they are

better than anybody else! Back then I will admit that I was slightly jealous of Jada

because she had everything that I wanted. She was drop dead gorgeous with long

hair, grey eyes, a nice car, and her parents had money so she didn't want for shit!

I didn't have a pot to piss in at the time and to have her look down her nose at me

cause me to feel about her the way that I do.

The sound of the front door slamming interrupts my thoughts and causes

me to jump. I poke my head out of the shower and yell. "Who's that?"

"Me. Who else has a key to your apartment?" Rodney replies.

"You don't have to get smart." I say rolling my eyes and smacking my lips! I

start to wash up.

He comes into the bathroom. "I need you to go back out to Marigold for

me. I've already put the stuff in the trunk of your car. You can just drop my half of

the money off with Demetrius when you get back because I have some shit that I

need take care of and I'll be out of town for a couple of days. I owe Demetrius

some money so that should take care of him."

I turn off the shower and step out. "Can you hand me my towel please?" He hands me my towel from the towel rack. "Yeah, I can go out to VA for you. Why are you going out of town and when are we going to spend some time together? It's beginning to feel like we are business partners rather than boyfriend and girlfriend."

"I told you that I have some business to handle out of town." He says. I notice that he is looking everywhere but at me. "We can do something when I get back."

I wrap the towel around my body and walk out of the bathroom. He follows me into the bedroom. "Is there a problem between us that you are not telling me about? I feel like I am missing something. I thought that we had squashed the little situation that happened between us."

"We have." He is sitting in the chair over in the corner watching me get dressed.

I look over at him and can tell by the way that he is looking at me that shit isn't one hundred percent between us. "Really? Well how come you haven't touched me lately? You came over the other night and you didn't even get undressed. You lay on top of the covers fully dressed. What's that about? I know how much you love pussy so something isn't right. Is there another bitch?"

He lets out a sarcastic chuckle while running his hands over his full beard. "Nah baby girl, there isn't another *bitch*. I've just been chillin'."

"Hmph...okay chillin'." I pull my lime green and black Coogie shirt over my head. "If you say so." He is still laughing. "What's so funny?"

"What happened last night?" he asks.

"Huh? What do you mean?" I am completely thrown off by his question.

"You heard me. I asked you, what happened last night or should I say this morning? Didn't you and some bitch named Jada get into an argument over your boy?" My mind is racing and I am wondering how in the hell he found out about that. "What's wrong? Cat got your tongue?"

"Nah...ummm...it wasn't over Shad." I am trying to think of something quick because I already know what he's thinking. This is the second incident that he's heard about with me and Jada getting into it. "That bitch had been drinking and was trippin'! You know how some bitches can't handle their liquor!"

"Oh damn, that's funny because the person that told me about it said that ol' girl hadn't said anything to you! They said that you started with her!" He is looking at me like I am transparent and he can see right through my ass!

"Ugggh...motherfuckas kill me running back telling shit and not telling it how it was!" I fume banging the brush that I was brushing my hair with on the dresser! "I hadn't said shit to that girl! Why are people always lying on Meechie! That shit is in the way! For real!"

Rodney gets up and come over to where I am standing. "It's cool Meechie, I know what time it is but remember what I told you, as long as you act like a trick that's how I am going to treat you!"

"Is that why you have me delivering dope for you?" I explode!

"Nah, I have you delivering dope for me so that you can pay your fuckin' rent! What you was thinkin' that I was some punk ass motherfuckas with blinders on that you could just use? I told you a long time ago that I ain't no sucka type nigga! You run your fuckin' mouth way too much!" I look at him confused. "Don't look stupid I overheard that shit you were saying on the phone when we were in Miami. How you weren't trying to do the love thing anymore, how you felt like I was obligated to take care of you because you were fuckin' me, and how you had no plans on going back to school or gettin' a job! You got me fucked up for real! Hearing that shit changed the game for us and then this shit with you and ol' girl! You swear up and down that you don't want Shad but this nigga's name is always coming up! You stay somewhere fuckin' with his girl! It sounds to me like you want that nigga but you just want to spend my money! You were never here for me from day one! It's been all about the paper! On some real shit I was really feeling you at first until you kept constantly showing me that you weren't about shit! I used to think that you deserved better than Shad but shit from where I'm standing that nigga deserves better than you! So with all of that being said I guess our shit has been reduced to business partners because you don't know shit about being any other type of partner! It's been about business for you since day one so I've just decided to make the best out of it! I ain't mad at you though, you saw a come up and you decided to run with it! I can't do shit but respect that!"

When he finally stops talking all I can say is. "So what are you saying?"

"I'm saying that I need you to make this run for me and drop my half of the money off at Demetrius' crib! I'll holla at you some other time. I've got shit to do." He slips on his shades and start to stroll out of the room.

"Rodney wait." I call after him. He stops and peers over his shades at me. "What about my car?" Shit, he's already told me there really ain't shit popping between us anymore so there ain't no sense in me begging and pleading with him! Fuck that! Like I said...I have a plan.

He reaches in his pocket and takes out his keys. He takes a single key off of the ring, tosses it at me and I catch it. "Hope you can afford to pay the note every month!" He walks out without another word. I finish brushing my hair back into a ponytail. I'm not the least bit sad about what just happened between Rodney and I. Fuck him! Like I said when we were in Miami, love don't live here anymore! I'm all about getting paper fuck everything else because love doesn't pay no damn bills!

I arrive at Douglas' house a little after four that afternoon. I grab the picnic basket from my trunk and walk up on the porch. I ring the bell and his housekeeper, Cynthia answers the door. "Good evening Meechie. Douglas has been expecting you. He's out on the sundeck, follow me." I follow her through the house and out onto the sundeck. I've never been out here before. The backyard is so beautiful! He has a big ass pool! There is a little bar set up on the deck! I could get used to some shit like this! There are a few people out by the pool, the grill is

216

going and music is playing. It looks like he is having a small get together. He is sitting in a chair on the porch dressed in a white linen pants suit holding some type of mixed drink. When I walk out onto the deck a wide smile forms on his lips and he stands to greet me.

"Hello beautiful." He says giving me a small peck on the cheek and at the same time taking the basket from my hands. "Here you go Cynthia, take this inside for me and bring back the envelope that is lying in my study on the desk." He gives her instructions. She nods and then disappears inside the house. "Have a seat." He offers.

I sit down in the seat next to him. He takes his seat, "Would you care for something to drink?"

"Sure." I accept. "Do you have any peach Absolute?"

"Sure do. Would you like it straight or mixed?"

"Straight with ice."

"Tony!" He calls and the dark haired white guy who has been tending the grill looks up.

"Yes sir."

"Can you fix my lady friend here a drink? She'd like peach Absolute on ice."

"Sure no problem."

Cynthia returns with the envelope and hands it to Douglas. He hands it to me. "Your basket will be inside when you're ready to go." She says.

"Okay."

"So how have you been beautiful?" Douglas asks smiling at me.

"I've been fine. How about you?" I ask looking at him really good, wondering if I can really go through with what I have planned. *Can I really see myself with this old fuck?* I wonder to myself. *He isn't ugly; maybe it won't be so bad. I may actually end up really feeling him.* Tony comes over and hands me my drink. "Thank you." I say taking a sip.

"You're welcome."

"I've been good but I could always be better." Douglas looks at me seductively. Then out of nowhere he starts to sing. *"I'm a movement by myself but I'm a force when we're together. You could make me better!"*

I am unable to contain my laughter. "Oh my goodness!" I continue you laughing at his attempt to flatter me by singing some Ne-Yo.

"What? You didn't think this *old man* knew anything about that did you?" he is laughing also. "You need to stop playing with that little boy you have and give this old man a chance. I can make you happy. I am sure of that. I'm not saying this to try and get you in bed or anything like that. I just find you to be very attractive and would love the opportunity to get to know you a lot better. Plus, I don't agree with your little gig that you have here. A beautiful woman such as ya'self shouldn't be delivering dope. You're worth way more than that. Have you ever thought about what would happen if you got caught?" I simply nod. "You don't want to end up giving years of your life to the system that you can never get back."

"Nah, I don't." I go into game mode. "It's just that I lost my job and I've been trying to find something else but I haven't had any luck. I don't want to lose my apartment or my car! Rodney gives me half of the money that I get from you and that is how I am able to keep my bills paid."

"You won't have to worry about any of that. I can finish paying for your car and pay your rent up for a whole year or you can give up your place and stay here. There's plenty of room."

He must think I'm stupid! I'm not giving up my place to move in with no man because whenever he gets on my damn nerves I can always take my black ass home! "I want to keep my own place."

He nods. "Okay, I tell you how we can do this. How about you spend a little time here with me, getting to know me better and we can go from there. I am going to have a few friends over tonight and I would love for you to stay."

"Sounds like a plan." I respond sipping my drink.

Rodney

I leave Meechie's crib, feeling some type of way. I really wanted to put my hands on her again but I know that I did the right thing by just walking out! I wonder how the fuck she thinks it made me feel when one of my boys called me this morning and told me that her trifling ass was outside of the club this morning arguing with Shad's girl over him. That bitch is just trifling! I notice that my car is almost on empty so I stop at the Shell store to get some gas. When I walk inside the first person I see is Shad. He is in line at the register. I'm ready to squash all of the dumb shit and air shit out between us! "Yo, what's up?" I approach him. "Can I holla at you for a minute outside before you leave?"

He is grilling me like he thinks that I am approaching him on some dumb shit! "Yeah...you can holla at me."

"Alright, let me pay for my gas." When I get outside he is standing on the sidewalk in front of the store. "I just wanted to holla at you and let you know that I don't have any beef with you..."

"Why would you?" He asks his eyes locked on mine.

"I'm just saying I know the situation with me and Meechie..."

"Look on some real shit, I don't have time to walk around here beefing with you over no female...point blank. She chose you so it is what it is! You didn't kidnap her, she went willingly!"

I nod my head. "True."

"The only shit that got to me about the whole thing is that we are blood but at the end of the day that shit really doesn't mean anything! I appreciate you coming to me and everything but I'm good!" He starts to walk off but then stop. "Oh before I forget, there is one thing that I wanted to let you know. I saw Meechie about a week ago and she had a bruise on the side of her face. She said that y'all were playing but I don't believe that shit! I understand that she's your girl and all now but putting your hands on her..." He shakes his head. "Nah bruh, that shit ain't what's up! You are a man not a bitch so if she makes you that upset to the point where you feel the need to put your hands on her. You need to walk away or leave her alone because the next time that I see a bruise on her face we will have beef and I honestly don't give a fuck if y'all are playing or not!" This nigga walks off like I'm some bitch that he can just check or something! I want to go after him and fuck him up but I already have a lot of shit going on! I decide to let him have this one!

I pump my gas, then get in my car and call Tia. The phone rings several times before she picks up. "Hello." Her sweet voice pours through the phone. Immediately all thoughts of Shad's bitch ass are replaced by sweet one's her. I am really digging her a lot. She's young but I enjoy spending time with her. We are going out of town today for a while just to chill and spend some time together. Neither of us wants to be seen in JC together because we both know how people around here talk which will only lead to a lot of drama that her or I don't need. She has warned me that she has an older brother who is very protective over her. I don't want to have to end up fuckin' that nigga up!

"So what's up are we still on for today?" I ask her.

"Yeah, you can pick me up from the park over on Pine St." She replies.

"Baby girl, why does it always feel like I am helping you sneak away from home or something?" I joke but there is some seriousness to my question. I've never picked her up from her crib. She's told me that she lives in the projects over on Parker St. but I don't even know which building.

"Nah, it ain't that but I've told you that my mama is really strict, she doesn't give a damn about me being eighteen. My brother is even worse!" She says.

I put on my signal and turn onto Pine St. "I am turning onto Pine St. now." I tell her. "I can't wait to see your fine ass."

"Awwww...I can't wait to see you either boo." I can hear the smile in her voice and imagine the sexy smile that she is wearing on her lips. I pull up next to the curb in front of the park. "I see you." I look up and see her jogging towards the car with a book bag on her back, a pocketbook dangling from her arm and her cell pressed against her ear. I watch as her full C cups jiggle as she jogs towards the car. When she reaches the car she opens the back door and throws her bags in the backseat and then slides in the passenger seat next to me. "Hey you." She leans over and kisses me. I can taste her bubble gum flavored lip gloss.

"Mmmmm...damn your lips are sweet." I lean over and get another kiss before putting the car in drive and pulling away from the curb. "So I was thinking that maybe we could spend the day in Ruby, VA. That's like an hour away. We could go out there and get a room, go out to eat, catch a movie, maybe do a little bit of shopping. It's whatever you want to do."

She reclines her seat a little and looks over at me. "We can do whatever as long as I'm with you it doesn't matter. We could just get a room and chill inside for the entire day if you want. You don't have to spend a lot of money for us to have a good time." She winks and blows me a kiss.

My soldier immediately stands at attention as I imagine her sweet lips wrapped around my dick. *Damn shorty bad!* I want this girl so bad that I can barely control myself. I reach over and caress one of her breasts. She bites on her bottom lip and makes a sexy face. "Damn you bad baby!" I compliment her.

"You have no idea!" She giggles. "What do you have good?"

"Look in the ashtray." I reply turning up the radio. Biggie's Big Poppa pours from the speakers as she gets the blunt from the ashtray and pushes in the lighter. She dances and snaps her fingers, rapping along with the lyrics. The lighter pops out and she touches it to the end of the blunt. She takes a long pull and inhales the smoke before placing the lighter back in the socket. She hits the blunt again and began to cough before passing it to me.

"Damn that shit is fiyah!" She coughs referring to the weed.

"Only the best baby when you're rolling with me." We pump Biggie and get high all the way to Ruby. When we arrive I get us a room at the Hyatt Hotel and carry our bags inside. Inside the room Tia takes off her shoes and get comfortable. Her cell has been blowing up the entire drive. She picks it up, powers it off and tosses it on the dresser.

"That must be your nigga trying to get in touch with you!" I tease as I take off my shoes and lay back on the bed getting comfortable. I pull my Polo over my head and toss it over on the chair.

"Nah, that's my mama. I am supposed to be in school but fuck that shit! School is for whack motherfuckas!" She giggles. "It's safe to assume that the school has called and informed her that I'm not there."

"Yo Lil' Mama on some real shit you need to have your ass in school! I didn't know that you were skipping school! I assumed that you were finished!" I am a little upset that she is ditching school! I mean I enjoy kicking it with her but I don't want her to be fucking up her education. "That shit ain't what's up!"

She turns around and looks at me with low eyes as a result of the kush that we've been smoking on. "Damn calm down! You over there tripping on me like you my daddy or something! School is boring to me so most of the times I just don't go! What's the big deal?"

"The big deal is that you really don't have shit if you don't have an education! Go to school shorty and get your education so that you can have something to fall back on. Being cute and stupid ain't a winning combination! A nigga want a woman who is fine but also has a good head on her shoulders!"

"Oh I have a good head on my shoulders!" She says with a devilish smile dancing on her lips. She walks over to where I am sitting on the bed and kisses me while unzipping my pants. I help her by lifting up so that she can pull them down some past my thighs. She leans down and takes the head of my Johnson inside of her warm wet mouth. She goes all the way down on it like a pro! I can feel her gagging she comes up and spits on the head of it and then go all the way down again until she is gagging again. She gets it all sloppy and wet. The slurping noises that she's making, mixed together with moans is driving me crazy! I feel the skin around my sac starting to tighten.

"Damn baby you have me ready to bust!" I grunt as she continues sucking my dick like it's her favorite flavor lollipop!

"Mmmm...go ahead and give me that cum!" She moans jacking my dick with her hand. She sticks out her tongue and licks the head. "Mmmm...I want you to cum in my mouth. Let me swallow your babies daddy." She takes me back in her mouth and within seconds I am shooting my load down her throat. She sucks me until I am dry and then sits up and wipes her mouth with the back of her hand. "Mmmm that was tasty!"

I sit on the bed trying to recover from the orgasm that I just had. This young freak just sucked my dick better than any bitch that I've ever fucked with. "Damn you sure as hell do have a good head on your shoulders!" I say looking at her shaking my head. "Damn..." I run my hand over my face.

She stands beside the bed and undresses slowly all the while looking at me. "You haven't seen nothing yet!" She lies down on the other end of the bed and spread her legs revealing a clean shaven snatch. She has one hand playing with her breasts and the other one between her legs playing in her pussy. "Mmmm...do you like what you see?" She moans. "Look how wet my pussy is for you." My dick is starting to come back to life. I stand up and undress never taking my eyes off of her. Her body is flawless! She has hers locked on mine. She removes her fingers from between her legs and put them up to her mouth. She sucks each one slowly. My hand is slowly stroking my hard on. "This pussy tastes so good. You want to taste it?" I've never been crazy about eating pussy but I feel like she has me in a trance or something. I get back on the bed and bury my face in her sopping wet snatch. "Mmmm...yes...eat this young tight pussy baby." She moans grinding her hips. I have to admit her juices taste like nothing else I've ever tasted. I am sucking on her clit causing her to squeal and moan loudly. "Oh god yes! Yes baby...suck that shit!" It isn't long before her legs are shaking and she is yelling out "daddy". Without thinking I crawl over top of her and plunge my dick as deep inside of her as it will go! She lets out a loud scream and I cover her mouth with mines as I continue to thrust in and out of her. Her pussy feel so good that I wish that I could stay inside of her forever but I know that is impossible because I feel myself about to let go again. I try my best to hold on longer but lose the battle and erupt inside of her!

The next afternoon Tia and I are on our way back to JC. She's lying in the passenger seat sleeping because we've been up all night fucking and smoking. I have the music turned up and the air blasting so that I can stay awake. My cell phone starts to ring, its Demetrius. I turn down the music and press send. "What's good my nigga."

"Hey man, I've been trying to reach you since last night!" he says the weightiness in his voice tells me that something is up. "Yo, I seen that nigga Crawl last night! He tried to pop some shit! I had Rolo and Craig with me. He had his girl with him but he made it clear that he would be seeing me again. He kept saying, 'I got something for you and your boy!' I told him that we could do it then but we were at the store over on Grant Avenue. He was like, 'I'll see both of y'all another time!' I don't know what that nigga is up too but I just wanted to let you know to keep your eyes open. Last night he knew that he was outnumbered but I wouldn't have been on no jumping shit and I told him so!"

"Fuck that nigga! I ain't thinking about that shit that he's talking! I haven't been hiding. If he wants me he knows where I be!" I roar into the phone causing Tia to stir in her sleep! "I ain't about to be walking around looking over my shoulder! It is what it is! He ain't really trying to do shit but a lot of talking because that shit that happened between us is like two months old!"

"Yeah but you never know man. I am just calling to warn you."

"I preciate' it but I ain't thinking about that bullshit! The next time that I see him there ain't going to be no fist fighting! The next time somebody is leaving the scene in a body bag!"

"I feel you. Just be careful."

"Always." I assure him. "I seen that nigga Shad yesterday morning. I tried to be on some peace type shit and squash whatever problems that we have between us. He was like he didn't have no beef with me and that the situation is what it is but then he tried to pop some shit about Meechie having a bruise on her face when he saw her. He was like if he sees another bruise on her then we would have problems. Man, I started to drop that nigga right then and there but I let it fly! I'm tellin' you, these niggas better get dey minds right before I end up fuckin' somebody up!"

"Don't let that shit get to you!" he tells me. "Where you at anyways?"

"On my way back to JC."

"That's what it is then. Just hit me up when you get back in town."

"Alright." We hang up and I tap Tia. "Wake up Lil' Mama."

Her eyes flutter open and she looks over at me. "What?"

"What are you going to do? Are you going home or back to my crib?"

"I'm rolling with you. I'll go home tomorrow. I don't feel like hearing my mama's mouth today. I'm too sleepy to deal with her." She closes her eyes and move around trying to get comfortable.

I am cool with that because I want some more of what she possesses between those sweet thighs of hers. I turn the radio back up and smile as I think about all the freaky shit that is about to go down later after I get some sleep.

Shad

It has been over a week since I last talked to Jada and come to think of it, I haven't heard anything from Meechie either! I've called Meechie several times and even left messages for her asking why she hasn't returned the car. This walking and catching rides shit ain't what's up!

It's Saturday and for the first time in a long time I have the day off from both jobs. I've been lying in bed for most of the day. It's now a little after one. I get up, take a shower and get dressed in a pair of black jean Roca Wear shorts, a white wife beater and a pair of black/white Jordans that I bought while Jada and I were at the mall a couple weeks ago. When I am done getting dress, I walk over to my ma's crib. I knock on the door a few times before she answers wearing a worried expression with a Newport dangling between her lips. She still has on her pajamas and her hair is wrapped up, which is odd for her because normally she'd be dressed by this time on a Saturday about to go play cards at her buddy Ms. Yvette's house.

"Hey stanger." She greets me stepping back out of the way to let me in. "I'm surprised to see you!"

I walk in and take a seat on the sofa. "I be working so much that I don't have time to visit like I want to." I explain. I am concerned as to why she looks so down. I know my mama like the back of my hand and I can tell that something is bothering her. "How have you been doing?"

"I've been making it. These bills are kicking my ass and that grown ass sister of yours is about to worry me half to death!"

I ignore her complaint about the bills and inquire more about what is going on with Tia. "Where is she at?"

"Hmmm...you're asking the wrong damn one! I haven't seen her ass since Thursday morning when she left here for school! I can't wait until she gets her lil ass back here though! I am going to go upside her damn head!" Her leg is bouncing up and down; this is something that she does when she is pissed. She takes a long pull off of her cigarette and then releases the smoke through her nose before putting it out in the ashtray. "The school called me around 11:00 Thursday and asked me why she wasn't at school. I told them that's where she was supposed to be. The principal informed me that the only day she'd been to school this week was Tuesday. Boy, I'll tell you that girl is going to make me put my foot in her ass! I have been calling her phone since Thursday morning but I haven't been getting anything but her voicemail!"

"That's if I don't get to her ass first!" I correct her! "What the fuck is wrong with her, not coming home and skipping school?" Hearing this has me beyond heated! As soon as I lay eyes on her I am going to fuck her up on sight! She knows better than this! I take out my cell and dial her number but just like ma said it doesn't even ring it goes straight to her voicemail! I leave a message telling her that she needs to bring her ass home immediately!

We both sit in silence for a few minutes, consumed by our own thoughts. I am trying hard to figure out where Tia might be but I am drawing a blank. Ma is the first to speak, "If she doesn't show up by the end of the day I am going to call the police. I'm praying that she's al..right." her voice cracks and I see the tears in her eyes.

I get up and walk over to her. I sit down on the arm of her chair and wrap my arms around her. "Don't cry ma, she's okay. Don't think negative, try to stay positive. She's just done got grown as hell and feeling herself! She'll turn up soon." I try my best to console her as best I can even though I am worried myself. I feel her tears wetting my arm.

"I just don't know what in the world I would do if something happens to her. She's just a baby for goodness sake! I try to give her freedom and not be hard on her because I have been her age and I know how it is. She's at the age now where she wants to hang out with her friends and talk to boys. I understand that but this right here..." She shakes her head. "I can't deal with this!"

"I know ma." I break our embrace and wipe her tears away with my hand. I get up and walk outside. I need some air this shit is too much for me to deal with! *God please let Tia be alright!* I take out my cell and call Jada. Somehow I feel that hearing her voice will make me feel better. The phone rings twice before she answers.

"Hello."

I detect a little attitude in her tone. "Hey, are you busy?"

"Yeah, I'm at work." She's being really short with me.

"Listen, I know that you are upset with me and I've thought about the things that you said and I understand where you are coming from. I apologize and I hope that we can move past this because right now I really need you."

"Oh so you called to apologize because you need a favor?" She laughs sarcastically. "Call Meechie..."

"Jada, my sister has been missing since Thursday, my ma just now told me! I called you because this shit has me kind of fucked up but I see that you are still on that bullshit about Meechie! I didn't let her use the car on no lovey-dovey type shit! As a matter of fact, I wasn't going to give it to her at first because like you said she only comes around when her ass needs something. I ain't slow, I see that shit! What made me change my mind was when I noticed that she had a bruise on her face. I asked her what happened and she shot me some bullshit about her and Rodney playing and he hit her too hard. I could tell she was lying. I know that nigga put his hands on her!" I paused to gather my thoughts. "I know that I shouldn't give a fuck but I can't lie to you, the thought of him putting his hands on her made me want to go and fuck him up! I know Meechie has some fucked up ways and I realize that she put herself in that situation but that still doesn't give him the right to be hitting on her. That shit really bothered me because on some real shit I still love her, not like I want to be with her but I was with her for over five years! You don't just stop giving a fuck about somebody that you were with that long overnight! Seeing that bruise on her face made me let my guard down so I went ahead and let her get the car. Just because she is fucked up doesn't mean that I have to be. I ain't that type of nigga! Like I told you that day in your car, I would've done the same thing for you."

She is quiet for a while and I hear her let out a sigh. "Shad, I wasn't thinking that you did it because you wanted her back. I am simply trying to get you to understand that at some point you have to let go and stop trying to always be there to catch her when she falls. Like you said she chose that situation that she is in! You didn't choose that for her! You have gone out of your way for this girl and in the end she always shits on you! When is enough going to be enough? Not only that but what woman do you know who is going to be willing to stick around while you are always running to Meechie's rescue? Maybe if she wasn't the type of person that she is, I could be more understanding but she is simply a hot ass mess! I wasn't going to say anything to you about this because I don't want it to seem like all I do is run back and tell you stuff instead of handling my own business but I saw Meechie the other night at Changez. Zy and I had gone out because I was upset about how things are between you and me. I was trying to have a little fun and get you off of my mind. Everything was good up until it was time to leave. I was standing outside waiting on Zy because she was talking to some dude. Meechie and her little crew spotted me and started trying to be funny. They were standing right next to me talking shit about me! Saying how you didn't want me and how I am only a fill-in because your heart still belongs to her. She even had the nerve to say that whenever she calls you are always going to come running! I got fed up and we almost got into it but of course the bouncers grabbed us and threatened to call the police if we didn't leave! Shad, I am not used to this kind of drama in my life and that is why I told you that if you continue to deal with Meechie then I have to stop dealing with you!"

I listen to everything that she has to say before I respond. "I understand where you are coming from. I apologize for you having to go through that bullshit but I promise that you don't have to worry about it anymore." I guarantee her. She's right there is entirely too much of Meechie and this shit has to stop! I can't allow her to come between me and Jada when I already know that at the end of the day in her world everything is all about her. I can never call on her when I need something or somebody to be there for my black ass but when I call on Jada, she's always there! It's about time that I handle my business but first I have to concentrate on finding my hot ass sister! "I know that you said that you were busy but I would really appreciate it if you would come through when you get off from work."

"I'll be over in a little while." She replies.

"That's what's up. I'll probably still be over at my mama's if Tia hasn't shown up."

"Alright...keep me posted and let me know if she shows up before I get there. I will keep my eyes open for her as well. Try not worry and pray that she returns home safely. I will do the same."

I smile at her comforting words. "Thanks baby."

"No problem...that's what I'm here for."

"Alright, I'll see you when you get here."

"Okay...Shad...I love you." She blurts. "I don't want you to say it back because I know that it's not how you feel right now. I just wanted you to know that is how I feel." She hangs up before I can say anything, which is good because I am not sure of how to respond to what she has just said.

I put my phone back in my pocket and go back inside with my mama to wait and see if Tia will show up.

Meechie

I've been laid up at Douglas' house for the past few days and it's been cool. Everything but the sex that it is! I am totally grossed out by his old ass but the up side is that it doesn't last that long. He's freaky though, he has been asking me to masturbate with toys while he watches and plays with his little shriveled up penis. To keep from throwing up I close my eyes tight and imagine that instead of him it's Rodney or either Shad. That is the only thing that gets me through it!

I've learned a few things about Douglas since I've been here. He's a really nice guy and he's really funny. If he was a few years younger we may be could have something real but I just can't get over the age difference. Being with him is like fucking my granddaddy! The most important thing has been that he lied about not getting high. He told the truth about him having it for his guests but since I've been here he's had two get-togethers and at both of them he was shoveling just as much powder up his nose as his guests! He even had the nerve to offer me some! I kindly declined because that isn't how I roll. I'll smoke a little kush but ain't shit going up my nose!

I've also been doing a lot of thinking since I've been here. If I can hang in here long enough with his old ass and get him to fall for me. I could get him to put me in his will and when his ass croaks all of this will be mine! He can't have much longer; between a heart attack and a drug overdose I believe that his days are numbered! I know my way of thinking may be harsh but I have to think long term! I ain't trying to be like some of these chics out here hopping from man to man to ensure that I am taken care of. I am trying to hit the jackpot so that I won't have to worry about hooking my next sucka and I can just concentrate on spending money and looking fly!

I look in the huge mirror above the bathroom sink and giggle at my thoughts as I am getting dressed to leave. When I am satisfied with my appearance I turn off the light and leave the bathroom.

I walk out into the bedroom. Douglas is sitting on side of the bed in a silk black robe. "I sure hate to see you leave beautiful." He says holding his arms open for me. I walk over to him and he wraps his arms around my waist. "I have enjoyed you so much these past few days." He confesses. "Have you enjoyed your stay here?"

"Yes, it's been nice." I admit truthfully because it has except for the sex. "I will be back in a couple of days though. I just have a few things to take care of at home."

He smiles up at me before kissing my exposed stomach. I am wearing a midriff top that shows of my sexy stomach. "I hope that you will come back and stay longer next time. I could get used to waking up looking at your beautiful face." He let's go of me and reaches over and opens the drawer on the nightstand. He pulls out a nice size white envelope and hands it to me. "Here this should be enough to take care of your rent for the rest of the year and enough to pay your car note for the next few months."

I take the envelope from his hand and hug him. "Thank you so much! Now how do you know that I will come back after you've given me all of this money?"

He laughs and caresses my ass through my tight blue jean shorts. "I'm more than certain that you will. I know your type and I know what it takes to keep you coming back." He winks at me.

I am not sure of the meaning of him comment but I brush it off and give him a light peck on the lips. "Well I am going to get on out of here. I will give you a call later."

He stands. "I'm going to walk you out beautiful." We walk outside to my car. I toss the picnic basket over in the passenger seat along with my pocketbook. "I didn't want to say anything but I know goodness well you don't have a note to pay off on this old raggedy car...no offense." He says referring to the Camry.

I shake my head. "No, this car right here is paid for. This is something that a friend of mine gave me to get around on while my other car was broken down."

"Oh okay." He opens the door for me, I get inside and he closes it. "Drive safely beautiful and call me later."

"I will." I start the car and put it in reverse. He blows me a kiss as I am backing out of the yard. I pretend to catch it. "Lame." I mumble. When I get to the end of his street, I reach over and grab the envelope that Douglas has just given me. There is nothing but crisp one hundred dollar bills. My hands began to tremble. I have never seen this much money in my entire life! "Gotdamnit! Meechie bitch you have definitely hit the motherfuckin' jackpot!" I yell to the top of my lungs! "I am about to shop until I motherfuckin' drop! I can't wait to see the look on Nikki and Carmen's faces when they see how I am ballin'! I know that them bitches are going to be mad and hatin' like nobody's business!" I laugh as I lean over and put the envelope in the glove box. *I think I may just call up Carmen and Nikki and invite them out just so I can rub my new found wealth in their faces!*

I grab my cell, plug it into my car charger and then power it on. My text messages notification goes off back to back for well over a minute and so does my voicemail notification. I start to drive again while dialing my voicemail, there are several messages from Shad asking about the car, a few from Carmen and Nikki asking where I am but none from Rodney. I dial Shad's number first. He picks up after several rings.

"Hello." His deep baritone voice comes through the phone.

"Hey, you've been trying to reach me?" I ask the dumb question knowing full and well that he has.

"Yeah, I have. I've been trying to find out what's up with the car? Have you gotten your car fixed yet or found a job? I ain't trying t be funny or nothing but this walking shit is getting old!"

"Yeah, I got my car fixed but no luck on finding a job." I lie. "Where are you now? I could bring the car to you but you will have to take me home."

"I'm over at my mama's house."

"Alright. I will be over there in about fifteen minutes." We hang up and I dial Rodney. His phone doesn't even ring, the voicemail automatically picks up. I dial him again but again I get his voicemail. Agitated that he isn't answering I toss my phone over in the passenger seat. I really just want to talk to him so I can tell him that his services are no longer needed and that he can kiss my pretty black ass! I also want to tell him where he can shove his dope because my days of delivering that shit are officially over!

When I get to Shad mama's house I pull up in front of her apartment and blow the horn. A few seconds later Shad comes out. *Damn!* I mumble as I watch him walking towards the car. He looks good enough to eat! I feel my pussy start to juice up as I think back to how he used to beat it up! *Whew! Damn Meechie stay focused! Good dick doesn't pay the bills either!* He reaches the car and I take my things out of the passenger seat and throw them in the back. He slides into the passenger seat.

"What's up?" he greets me.

"Hey." I put the car in reverse and back up. As we are driving to my house the car is silent. I am guessing that things have been so crazy that neither of us know what to say to each other. "Thanks for letting me use the car."

"No problem." He replies continuing to look out at the streets as if he's searching for something.

"You sure are quiet. You can still talk to me you know, I don't bite." I laugh at my own joke but Shad still doesn't say anything. He just continues looking out at the street. He's looking as if he's visiting JC for the first time in his life! "Is something wrong?"

"Yeah, Tia hasn't been home in a few days and I am trying to keep an eye out in case I see her."

"Oh…" I am kind of relieved because I was thinking that maybe Jada had told him about what happened at the club. "I thought maybe you were upset with me about something."

He finally looks at me. "Nah, I don't have the time or the energy to walk around being mad at anybody. There's entirely too much other stuff that requires my time and energy. I don't have any to waste."

For some reason I am slightly offended by his response because it makes me feel like he's trying to say that I am not important enough for him to be wasting his energy on me. I glance over at him briefly, "What is that supposed to mean?"

"It means exactly what I said." He replies.

"Are you trying to tell me something on the low?"

"Nope! I am a grown man Meechie and if there is anything that I have to tell you I am man enough to tell you straight up without beating around the bush."

I turn into my complex. "Oh okay because you seem like you had something that you wanted to get off of your chest."

"Well I do but it has nothing to do with anything that you are talking about because I am not mad with anybody."

I park in the empty parking space next to my Nissan and turn off the ignition. "Alright well speak your mind." I say turning to him giving him my undivided attention.

He looks me directly in my eyes and began to speak. "You made the decision months ago to walk away from our relationship because you were unhappy. I didn't agree with your reasons and to be honest I still don't. To me it was fucked up the way that you did things but it is what it is. With that being said, you've move on with someone new and so have I. I believe it's time for me to cut off all communication with you and allow the past to be the past, which means I don't want you popping up at my job or calling my phone. Whatever problems that you have you will have to deal with them on your own because I can no longer be there to help you. I'd also appreciate it if you'd stop harassing Jada everywhere that you see her. I don't understand your reasoning behind it if you have moved on with somebody else. I just want to move on from all of the drama and be happy. I wish you the best in whatever..."

I've heard enough of this bullshit! "Nigga what the fuck do you mean, don't be calling your phone or popping up at your job?" I explode! I knew that Jada's ass had run back and told him about the other night! This time I am definitely going to whoop her ass! "Oh so that's how you are going to play me for that bitch?"

He's giving me an agitated look. "I am going to play you like this because of you! Not Jada but you! You need to grow up Meechie! Nobody has time for all of the drama and bullshit! I certainly don't! You said that you were done with me and had found a man better than me so that's what it is! All I ask is that you leave me and my girl alone! That's it! Is that too much to ask for? I don't come around starting shit with Rodney or you! Do I?"

I get out of the car slamming the door! I open the backdoor and grab my pocketbook tossing it on my shoulder! "Fuck you Shad! You and your bitch! I got something for her ass though! She was so bad talking shit the other night but then gone run back and tell you just like I knew she would!" I am fuming mad! "You don't even want that bitch like that! I know that you are only fucking with her to get back at me for fucking with Rodney!"

"Damn is that what you believe?" He asks getting out of the car and walking around to the driver's side to get in. "I'm sorry to deflate your big ass ego but me being with Jada doesn't have shit to do with you or Rodney! Just do as I asked and leave her alone. If she isn't fucking with you then don't fuck with her!"

"I will do whatever the fuck I want as a matter of fact I am going to get in my car right now and go down to her little bouji ass café! Since that bitch got so much mouth! She said the last time that she was going to call the police well you had better call and tell her to have those motherfuckas waiting because that ass is mines today!"

This motherfucka has the audacity to laugh like I just said something funny. "Sometimes I wonder what I ever saw in you." With that he gets in the car and drives off!

Him driving off in my face like he just did only elevates my anger! I search through my pocketbook and find the keys to my car! I hit the button on the remote to unlock the doors and then get in tossing my pocketbook into the passenger seat. Tears burn my eyes. I am mad and at the same time hurt. I never saw that coming in a million years! *This bitch has convinced Shad to cut all ties with me! Who in the fuck does she think she is?* I think to myself as my tears start to wet my cheeks! I didn't think it would bother me this much to hear Shad say that he wanted nothing else to do with me! After all I was the one who walked away from him right? That was different though because even though I walked away from him, I knew that regardless of what he would always be there and I would always remain a part of his life...I am so upset and deep in thought that don't notice that the light is red or the truck that is coming!

Epilogue

Six months later...

Shad is sitting in the Camry parked in the driveway looking out across the yard at nothing in particular. His mind consume by thoughts of Tia, though six months has passed it all still seems surreal. His mind goes back to six months ago when he got the news.

Six months earlier...

Loud banging at the front door jerked Shad from his sleep! He hadn't been too long ago laid down on his mama's couch to get some rest. He'd been up all night after hearing the news that Meechie had been in a fatal accident that had claimed her life instantly. He'd rushed to the hospital hoping that she wasn't gone but when he got there and saw the condition that her family was in; he knew that she was indeed gone. Even though things hadn't been good between the two of them realizing that she was gone and he would never see her again hurt him o the core. There was no way that he could hold back the endless tears that poured from his eyes. He stayed there at the hospital with her mama trying his best to comfort her as much as possible but there wasn't much that he could do. When he'd finally made it back to his mama's house, sleep didn't come easy because every time that he closed his eyes he kept seeing Meechie and how upset she'd been when he'd left her.

The present day...

He jumped up from the sofa and ran to the door! Jada, who had been sleeping in the chair was also awakened and jumped up! Shad peeped through the peephole in the door and saw two police officers standing on the other side. A bad feeling formed in the pit of his stomach and somehow he knew that whatever they were about to tell him wasn't something that he was prepared to hear. By now his mama was on her way down the stairs, hoping that her baby had finally returned home.

Shad unlocked the door and snatched it opened. "Good morning." He greeted the officers.

"Good morning sir. We are looking for a Sharon Easton." The tall lanky officer informed him.

"Yes sir, I'm right here." Sharon said from behind Shad.

"What's wrong?" Shad asked unable to control his anxiety any longer. He knew that something was wrong with Tia but he was praying that it wasn't as bad as the feeling in his gut was telling him.

"Ma'am we found your daughter Sha'Tia Easton." He handed her the school ID that they'd found in Tia's pocketbook.

Sharon looked down at the ID and tried to take it but her hands were trembling too badly and her knees all of a sudden gave out. Shad caught her just before she hit the floor. "Is...she alright?" She asked barely above a whisper with her hand covering her mouth. Her eyes searching both of the officer's faces for some indication that her baby was okay but there was none. The sympathetic expressions on both of their faces told her that Tia wouldn't be returning home. "Please...tell me...that she's alright." She cried pleading with them.

"Ma'am, can we please come in?" The second officer who happened to be a brother that looked to be in his late thirties.

"No motherfuckas, you can't come in but you can tell us what the hell is wrong with my gotdamn sister!" Shad exploded! "Stop all of this motherfuckin prolonging!"

"Sir please calm down." The tall lanky officer pleaded with Shad.

Jada stepped in. "Shad, baby calm down. Step back out of the way and let them in." Shad reluctantly stepped back still holding on to his mama. The two officers came in and everyone took a seat.

The black officer spoke this time. "I hate to have to come and give you such bad news this morning but Sha'Tia's body was found along with a male this morning in a home at the 400 block of N. Winston St." Sharon let out a loud scream! Shad sat silently just shaking his head unable to believe what he'd just heard. Jada cried silently. "Both victims were shot multiple times. We do have a suspect in custody."

"Why God? Why my baby?" Sharon cried. The officers waited for Sharon to get herself together and then asked her if she could get dressed and follow them down to the coroner's office to positively identify the body.

After getting dressed, Jada drove Shad and Sharon down to the coroner's office where they identified Tia's body. That's when Shad lost it, after seeing Tia's body he could no longer control his emotions and proceeded to ransack the coroner's office. It took over ten minutes for the officers to calm him down. Later on at the police station was where Shad had received the biggest shocker! He found out that the male that Tia's body had been found with was Rodney. He'd tried his best to figure out how in the hell Tia had ended up with Rodney. The police explained that after going through her phone and reading text messages it was obvious that the two had been seeing each other. After hearing all of this Shad couldn't take anymore and walked out of the precinct!

Back to the present day...

Six months after lying to rest the first woman that he ever loved and his sister all in the same week, the pain is still damn near unbearable. A tear rolls down his cheek and he swipes it away. "I still can't believe that y'all are gone." He whispers referring to Tia and Meechie. "This shit just ain't right. I swear on everything I love they better hope they don't ever let that nigga Crawl out because if they do, I promise you Tia, I am going to take care of that nigga baby girl. I promise!" The tears continue to fall. "I was supposed to protect you and I didn't. I'm sorry Tia."

Jada looked out the window and saw Shad just sitting out in the car, which was something that he did a lot. She knew that he was having a hard time dealing with the loss of Tia and Meechie and she truly understood. She hated to see him like this but she was hoping that what she'd just found out a few minutes ago might lift his spirits. She grabbed her sweater from the coat rack by the door and walked out to the car. She opened the passenger door and got inside.

"Hey baby, what are you doing out here as cold as it is?" Shad asked her wiping his eyes.

"I came to check on you." She slid in the middle of the seat and wrapped her arms around him pulling him into her arms. He laid his head on her chest. "It's going to be okay baby. I know that it's hard right now but it'll get easier. You just have to pray and ask God to make it easier."

"I know baby but it just hurts so fuckin' bad! Tia didn't deserve that shit! She got killed all behind some shit that didn't even have shit to do with her! That ain't right Jada!" he cried.

"You're right baby but remember God doesn't make no mistakes. I know that you can't see that right now but everything happens for a reason."

Shad sat up shaking his head. "Nah, fuck that! God didn't have no hand in this shit! He wouldn't have taken my sister! She was just a baby...a fuckin' baby!"

Jada used her hand to wipe his tears. "We'll get through this together baby...all three of us."

"I know baby. I know that you and my mama are here for me. I appreciate y'all. I need to be being strong for my mama; instead she's been strong for me." He looked over at Jada through teary eyes. He was glad to have her by his side. She'd proven her love for him over the past six months she'd been by his side doing whatever she could to help him through this difficult time. Never once had she complained. "I love you woman."

"I love you too, *babydaddy*." She realized that her first hint had totally gone over his head so she decided to give it another try.

Shad looked at her confused. "Huh?"

"I said that I love you too babydaddy." She started to get emotional. She could still see that he was confused. "I'm pregnant Shad!"

"But...but...I thought that you couldn't get pregnant? How do you know? I mean when did you find out?" He asked not knowing exactly how to react.

"Well my little friend hasn't come in two months, the first month I thought that it was just stress but then when it didn't show up this month I decided to take a pregnancy test. I've taken three since last night and all three have been positive!"

Shad sat there and stared at her for a few seconds before he grabbed her and pulled her into his arms. "I love you girl! I am about to be a damn daddy!"

"Yeah, you are!" Jada giggled in his arms her tears wetting his shirt. "You're going to be a damn daddy!"

He broke their embrace and looked down at her. "Oh you got jokes?" He asked kissing her.

"No baby but it was kind of funny the way that you said it!"

He kissed her again. "Oh be quiet!"

"Do you have any napkins in your glove box?" She asked already opening it and looking inside. She didn't see any napkins but a white envelope fell out and money poured out onto the floor! "Oh shit! Shad!" She reached down scooping up all of the crisp one hundred dollar bills!

Shad looked over to see what she was yelling for and saw her holding two handfuls of money! "What in the...where did you get that from?"

"It fell out of an envelope that was in your glove box!" The two of them took the money inside the house and counted it. When they were done they'd counted twenty-thousand dollars.

Jada looked at Shad. "Where in the hell did Meechie get this kind of money from?" She knew that's where the money had to have come from because she was the only one who had been driving the car.

Shad was still in disbelief, he'd never seen this much money before in his entire life! "I have no idea baby."

"Well, I believe that us finding this money was a blessing. Now you can buy your shop!"

He looked at her. "Yeah, I guess you're right baby...I guess you're right."